OD for the Accidental Practitioner

"Written by two seasoned, experienced organization development professionals, this book will likely become a key resource for a group of people who, either by choice or circumstance, have become responsible for guiding learning and change in organizations. Kokkelenberg and Miller have done an extremely creditable job of outlining a complete curriculum for professional OD development."

**—Peter F. Norlin, PhD, Principal, ChangeGuides;
Former Executive Director, OD Network**

"*OD for the Accidental Practitioner* is clearly written and offers a great deal of wisdom for the 'accidental' OD practitioner, which actually is a much larger population than perhaps even the authors realize. Lawrence Kokkelenberg and Regan Miller have performed a valuable service by writing this book."

**—Todd L. Matthews, PhD, Professor and Chair, Department
of Leadership and Organization Development and Change,
Cabrini University**

"*OD for the Accidental Practitioner* is a comprehensive look at the field and practice of organization development, co-authored by two very experienced and deeply respected practitioners."

**—Dr. Kris Lea, PsyD OD, PCCP, President, Kris Lea Consulting
Group, Inc.**

"Kokkelenberg and Miller have written a straightforward account of organization development (OD), easy to read, clear to understand, useful to ponder. Written for 'accidental' practitioners from other fields who are doing OD for various reasons, the book is an informative and welcoming companion. A caring way to learn OD. For more 'seasoned' OD veterans, the book provides a rich array of insights and cases that rekindle one's own experiences and stimulate learning from them. An inspiring way to continue the journey."

—Thomas G. Cummings, Professor of Management and Organization, University of Southern California

"Having been an OD practitioner for almost fifty years, I found this book refreshing and a reminder of the OD concepts and beliefs I hold dear. This book is a must-read for accidental practitioners and those who have been practicing the craft of OD for years. As the authors said, practicing OD is both an art and a skill that requires a balance between how you like to engage with clients, your preferred approaches to whole system improvement, and the uniqueness of each and every client . . . a lesson that often takes practitioners years to understand. This book will speed up your learning process and for us old-timers remind us of why we have dedicated our lives to OD."

—Frederick A. Miller, CEO, The Kaleel Jamison Consulting Group, Inc., ODN Lifetime Achievement Award Recipient, Co-author of *Safe Enough to Soar: Introducing Interaction Safety*

"Practical. Useful. Down to earth. This is the book I wish I'd had when I first stumbled into the consulting profession. Larry and Regan have given us an informative, enlightening, and digestible handbook. Read it. Absorb it. Apply it. And pass it on to others."

—Dr. Karl Albrecht, Author of *Blueprint for a New America*

"This is an excellent, practical book that is based on the extensive practical experience of authors Kokkelenberg and Miller. The book is well written and covers the waterfront of change management, organization design, organization development, and so much more.

It is for anyone—OD consultants, managers, or even workers—who find themselves trying to facilitate change efforts in organizational settings. My advice: buy the book, read it, and apply what you learn from the wisdom contained in it."

—William J. Rothwell, PhD, SPHR, SHRM-SCP, CPLP Fellow, Professor, Penn State University/University Park

"It is true that most OD practitioners enter the field through a side door rather than the main entrance with a shiny new master's degree or doctorate. And most are expected to hit the ground running, learning as you go if necessary. Kokkelenberg and Miller have provided the consummate companion piece written with the inexperienced practitioner in mind. In fact, it might be a good idea for practitioners to download their copy into their iPhone."

—W. Warner Burke, PhD, Professor of Psychology and Education, Teachers College, Columbia University

"Organizations are operating in increasingly turbulent worlds that require them to navigate the complex dynamics of change. Kokkelenberg and Miller's clear and concise book, based on years of experience and packed with practical and psychological insights, is a timely resource for people wanting to understand what organization development (OD) is about, and how it can help their organization to thrive. The book's case examples, checklists, and 'wisdom bits' will be useful prompts for OD practitioners as they address their organizations' OD challenges in these radically changing times. It's a really good read."

—Dr. Linda Holbeche, Visiting Professor, OD and HRM, City of London University Business School

"I think it's important for those entering into the field of OD to gain an understanding of the history and purpose of OD, and how to transfer their current skills to become an experienced OD professional. I think this book will help the accidental practitioner understand how they can develop the competencies needed to effectively lead OD change initiatives."

—Dr. Nancy Zentis, CEO, Institute of Organization Development

"Larry and Regan have brought the principles and concepts of OD to life in practice. Few have approached understanding the field through the eyes of those who are practicing without the benefit (or restraints) of first learning it all through academic lenses. This book captures the essence of what is needed *by the practitioner* themselves, the organization, the foundations and processes of OD, and organization change. It also makes good connections with foundational theories and practices for added knowledge of readers. It's an excellent reminder for more experienced practitioners and a field book for new or accidental practitioners."

—David W. Jamieson, PhD, President, Jamieson Consulting Group, Inc.; Editor in Chief, *OD Review*

"I really enjoyed reading this book. It covers a broad range of theories, methodologies, tools, etc., to enable the reader to understand the many aspects of OD in a very clear and logical way. Although it is intended for the accidental practitioner, it is also useful for seasoned practitioners as a way of reconnecting to aspects of OD that may have been forgotten (or possibly lurk in the recesses of our minds). The structure includes case examples and study group or self-reflection questions at the end of chapters to facilitate the learning process. The definition of OD is simple but not simplistic—the essence of what OD is about."

—Glenda Hutchinson, Organization Development Consultant, IODA Co-Vice President of Conferences and Events

"There is a strong need for those new to the field of OD to have a resource for understanding and practicing sound and effective OD. This book responds to that need. However, it also goes beyond this need and offers practical ideas for seasoned practitioners as well."

—Dr. D. D. (Don) Warrick, Professor of Leadership and Organization Change and President's Teaching Scholar, University of Colorado, Colorado Springs

OD for the Accidental Practitioner:
A Book Written by Practitioners, for Practitioners

by Lawrence Kokkelenberg, PHD and Regan Miller, MS

ISBN 978-1-64663-625-9

Published by

 köehlerbooks ™

3705 Shore Drive
Virginia Beach, VA 23455
800-435-4811
www.koehlerbooks.com

OD

FOR THE

ACCIDENTAL PRACTITIONER

**A BOOK WRITTEN BY PRACTITIONERS,
FOR PRACTITIONERS**

LAWRENCE KOKKELENBERG, PHD
REGAN MILLER, MS

VIRGINIA BEACH
CAPE CHARLES

TABLE OF CONTENTS

Chapter 1: OD for the Accidental Practitioner 1

Acknowledgment 1

Purpose 2

Structure of the Book 4

Chapter 2: Organization Development Foundations 6

What is Organization Development? 6

Definition 8

Wave Theory 9

Top-Down Model 10

Where did OD Start? 13

Organization Development Models 15

Organization Design 18

Proactive Versus Reactive OD 19

OD in the Organization 21

Internal vs. External Practitioner 22

Discussion Questions. 25

Chapter 3: About the Practitioner 27

Introduction 27

Knowledgeable Practitioner vs. Skillful Practitioner 27

Competencies 28

Use of Self 30

Sensitivity to Self 32

Becoming Sensitive as a Form of Introspection 35

Positive Attitude/Disposition 36

Broaden and Build Theory 39

Emotional Competency 40

A Study in EI 42

Are Some Emotions Better Than Others? 44

Judgments 45

Values 47

Individual Values 47

Values Violation 49

Slippery Slope 49

Emotions and Values 51

Bias 52

Levels of Bias and Probability of Change 54

What Are My Preferences? 56

Conclusion 58

Discussion Questions 58

Chapter 4: About the Organization 59

Introduction 59

What is an Organization? 59

Defining Organization Design 60

Models in Organization Design 61

Understanding Organization Design
in Organization Development 62

Factors in Organization Design....................... 63

Organization Performance............................ 69

Systems Influence 70

Organization Climate................................ 74

Organizational Values 77

Conflict Style....................................... 79

Multiple Systems 80

Future of Organization Structures 84

Conclusion... 86

Discussion Questions................................ 87

Chapter 5: Organizational Change.................... 88

Introduction 88

Failed Initiatives 89

Client Readiness 95

Setting the Stage for Change....................... 98

Organizational Change 102

Resistance to Change 106

Red Lights 109

Root Cause....................................... 110

Common Root Causes 112

Cost of the Problem............................... 115

Turnover... 116

Design the Intervention/Training Program 118

Caution: Flavor of the Month...................... 118

Conclusion 119

Discussion Questions. 119

Chapter 6: Engaging in the OD Process **121**

Introduction 121

Phases in OD 122

"Who Is the Client?". 125

Diagnostic 128

Reporting Diagnostic Results 132

Design. 135

Develop. 139

Delivery 141

Project Completion. Exit Point. 142

Follow-Up and Evaluation. 143

Evaluating Different Organizations 144

Illegal Activities. 147

Consulting Elements 148

Problem-Solving and Decision-Making 148

Unintended Consequences. 149

Relationships. 150

Levels of Relationships 152

Leadership is About Relationship 153

Trust 155

Assessing Trust. 157

Teambuilding. 158

Group Dynamics 161

OD Practitioner Roles 163

Facilitation, Coaching, Advising 166

Training and Development 170

Does Training Really Benefit the Organization? 172

Developing Infrastructure 174

Discussion Questions. 177

Chapter 7: The Future of OD 179

Introduction 179

Factors Influencing OD 180

Change in World View 185

Bridging the Gap: Academia and Practitioners 188

Confusion in OD 188

Conclusion 189

Discussion Questions. 190

Chapter 8: Wisdom Bits 191

Introduction 191

Wisdom Bits. 193

Stories for Reinforcement 200

A Great Risk: Certified and Knowledgeable,
Far from Skillful. 200

The Value of the 80 Percent Concept. 202

Illegal, Ethical, Immoral. 203

References 207
About the Authors. 212

CHAPTER 1

OD for the Accidental Practitioner

ACKNOWLEDGMENT

We were fortunate to have careers that allowed us to go into other organizations and be exposed to different cultures, leadership styles, employees, working atmospheres, rules, and regulations, etc. This experience alone is an education. We got to see what works and why it works, or what is not working and the consequences of that. We were able to broaden our experiences as we helped organizations improve. We saw success and failure and what caused those results. We made mistakes, *often* at the clients' expense, and then learned from them. Every experience we were exposed to made us more knowledgeable and more skillful for the next client. We were fortunate to learn by doing and were exposed to a wide variety of projects and circumstances.

We are truly blessed to have had over two hundred of these opportunities to date. We are thankful to the companies that have engaged us, putting up with the miscues or misdirection any large initiative invariably has. We are thankful to the countless number of individuals who candidly poured out their hearts to us in the hopes that their honesty and openness would do some good and help to improve their organizations. We are thankful to the skeptics who alerted us to the problems we might not have seen and to show us the level of resistance that might have existed. They all played a valuable part in the change dynamic. We are thankful to thousands of employees who sat through our group sessions and training programs, who endured our humor and wisdom, and hopefully we journeyed together and learned from each other.

Additionally, we are thankful to the many individuals who agreed to review and provide feedback on our manuscript. Your critical feedback, additional ideas, and endorsements helped shape the book we share today.

PURPOSE

All of us live, work, and play in an organized society. There is no getting away from being involved in organizations, all of which influence our behaviors. Outside of work, there is the global society, the country society, the state society, and the community society, all of which we may not play a critical role in but are a part of. However, there is the family, church, professional/technical, and work society, all of which we might have extensive roles in. The OD practitioner is called upon to engage in and improve all levels of society, and this book is written for all practitioners at whatever level they choose to engage.

The idea for this book came about shortly after attending an OD conference where we recalled many attendees telling us they came into the field through a back or side door. That OD was not their chosen profession initially, that they were in other fields, and when the organization developed an OD position, they were either chosen to fill that position or applied because it seemed more interesting than what they were currently doing. As time goes on there may be more intentional practitioners who go to graduate school in the OD field, but at least for now, there are many organization development (OD) practitioners who emerge from other professional fields. Sometimes practitioners come from a background similar to OD (change management, training, human resources) and sometimes not (process improvement, engineering, etc.). Because OD practitioners are not required to attend schools or specific academic programs, or obtain certifications, the body of knowledge for an emerging practitioner can be obtained and practiced in many ways. If you find yourself in this situation, i.e., emerging into OD from another field, you may fit into the group we refer to as "accidental practitioners." This book is for you, the accidental practitioner. We also believe that practitioners without a lot of experience will find many helpful tips within these pages.

Practicing OD requires many skills that are learned through experience and time. Understanding the history of the field, theories on behavior and culture, organizational models, and intervention methods are important; this foundational knowledge, usually acquired academically, gives you tools to use when working with a client. However, practicing OD is both an art and a skill that requires a balance between how you like to engage with clients as a practitioner, your preferred approaches to whole system improvement, and the uniqueness of each and every client you will work with. This book is intended to provide the practitioner with the experiences of others and thought-provoking guidance when engaging with clients.

This book is written by practitioners for practitioners. Our goal is to provide insights and thought-provoking ideas on how to approach OD in any number of client organizations. The book is not intended to be a prescriptive approach (it does not advocate for a specific theoretical model or approach) or provide an academic overview of the field of OD. Rather it is to help guide your thinking, help develop your skills, and help broaden your knowledge as you practice OD. There are many readily available scholarly books published about organization development work, theories, models, approaches, etc., well documented and grounded in research findings with notations of authorship, often quoting past research and discussing comprehensive approaches to OD. This book is intended to be a concise, practical, useful, thought-provoking guide for practitioners.

STRUCTURE OF THE BOOK

While there are distinct, clear cut areas in this book, in practice there is often a flow between the areas. The line between the various stages of OD is very porous. The reader can choose to go through the chapters in order or pick relevant sections to explore. The following outlines the chapters and content:

Chapter Two: Organization Development Foundations. A brief history of OD, discussion of the top-down model and wave theory, introduction to OD models, and the difference between internal and external practitioners.

Chapter Three: The Practitioner. This chapter reviews the integral nature of the practitioner in the OD process. Discussion topics include the use-of-self and sub-topics that align to that (i.e., values, judgments, emotional intelligence, etc.).

Chapter Four: The Organization. Organizations are all unique. This chapter discusses foundational organization characteristics such as design, systems influence, culture, and other characteristics a practitioner may want to consider in any engagement.

Chapter Five: Organization Change. This chapter focuses on the challenges that occur during change processes, the process of change, and overcoming resistance to change.

Chapter Six: The Process and Organizational Factors. OD requires a systematic approach to navigating complex challenges. This chapter provides information on how to structure that process from the beginning of an engagement (contracting) to designing and developing interventions, and finally exit and evaluation. Also, this chapter discusses common factors where the practitioner may want to pay close attention, such as relationships, teamwork, and trust.

Chapter Seven: The Future of OD. The field of OD is evolving and will continue to evolve. This chapter discusses areas that influence the evolution and aspects of the field the authors are advancing for further consideration. The post-pandemic organization, or the new normal, will not mirror the old normal, and this alone will provide many challenges to relationships, leadership, organizational cultures, organization design, policies, missions, and many more areas.

Chapter Eight: Wisdom Bits. This section distills many OD concepts into simple-to-remember phrases that can help guide a practitioner through challenging work engagements. They are excellent reminders for motivating both practitioners and clients. They also can serve as excellent discussion questions and lead into numerous theories of OD.

CHAPTER TWO

Organization Development Foundations

WHAT IS ORGANIZATION DEVELOPMENT?

When designing this book, it became obvious that the text had to contain some description of organization development (OD). An accidental practitioner would reasonably need to know some foundational information about the field. How does the field define itself? Is it a practice, a profession, a science, a discipline, or a body of knowledge? What definition best captures the work of an OD practitioner? What characteristics (i.e., competencies, knowledge, traits, skills) would a practitioner have? While seemingly simple, these questions do not have readily available or consistent textbook answers. The field lacks a single governing body that guides all members under a united concept; as a result, it may appear confusing. Ultimately, this confusion has created fractions of varying professional groups, all with different interpretations and different approaches to OD. Perhaps after reading this book, you will make your own interpretations and your own way forward in the field. This book presents the authors' interpretation of what OD is and is not and is expected to continue the existing debates in hopes that one day, the field reaches agreement and unites behind common themes to create a cohesive, respected, and professional OD field of practice.

This book is titled *OD for the Accidental Practitioner* because so many practitioners emerge from other fields, some similar in focus or orientation such as human resources, training and development, change management, coaching, I/O psychology, and some more distant in orientation, such as engineering, operations, management, etc. As a result, the field is full of individuals that are trained in other areas of expertise who may or may not have gone through formal educational programs to learn the necessary body of knowledge or the history of OD. The emergence of practitioners from other fields presents great benefits to OD, such as practitioners who can speak the language of their customers or who understand elements of business and organizations from years of experience. However, this may also present disadvantages, in that anyone can ultimately call themselves an OD practitioner. Without a governing body that provides certification options, or clearly describes the characteristics and competencies of effective OD practitioners, we end up with an all-inclusive, vague, and hazy profession. This has and continues to cause confusion within the profession.

With all these variations in the field itself, we must look to history to find some context about what OD is. Many who are familiar with OD will point back to efficiency studies in the 1930s and 1940s, but still many others will point to the 1960s with the rise of self-examination and introspection or social movements of that era. Still, others will look back to the introduction of chaos theory and systems theory as the start of OD. For the practitioner, it will be beneficial to understand all of these theories and movements and their impact on organizations. They have all made contributions to the field and shaped where we are today. If nothing else, the evolution of these theories should convince the field to recognize its constant evolution. As people and organizations change, so will the field. OD must evolve with the changing nature of our social, economic, and political systems to support organizations most effectively.

DEFINITION

There have been many attempts at providing a concrete definition of organization development, and all are laudable. Part of the difficulty is that the field continues to evolve and expand. There are many important, necessary, and appropriate specializations in professions that work with organizations including team building, conflict resolution, management, and supervisory training, organization design, workforce planning, leadership development, and coaching; however, these are only a piece of what we call OD. The focus of these specializations is quite specific, while OD work is broad, encompassing the entire organization and all of its systems, policies, processes, people, history, culture, customers, etc.

All of these broad activities that are a part of OD make it difficult to construct an all-encompassing definition. An uncharacteristically simple yet comprehensive definition of OD emerged from a simple comment we heard from a senior manager at a large human resources consulting organization. When visiting school children, the question was asked, "What does your organization do?" and rather than give a long definition of the organization's mission statement, this individual simply said, "**We help people and organizations be better.**" This definition embodies the essence of what practitioners, academics, and researchers alike do. This definition is the driver for the concepts discussed in this book and is what we use to guide our OD work in organizations.

OD is a systems approach to diagnosing the health and functionality of an organization and the people within. This includes identifying and implementing interventions designed to positively influence that organization and ensuring the organization can successfully continue on its own in a healthy and efficient manner. OD is not simply serving as a facilitator, a training specialist, an HR professional, a coach, an I/O psychologist, a change management specialist, etc.; however, at any time, it may include some or all those elements.

WAVE THEORY

There are several fields of study that use wave theory.

- Physics: often referring to light passing through objects
- Finance: Elliott wave theory, referring to patterns often in the stock market
- Linguistics: in the development of a new language departing from its origins
- Military: a coordinated frontal assault with densely concentrated infantry

For purposes of this book, wave theory refers to human history and the major patterns therein.

The first wave: nomadic and independent living. For millennia, humans were nomadic, and food came mainly from animals. In all that time, people learned that hunting in groups or tribes was better than hunting alone. In this lifestyle, people also had to migrate with the animals or starve. Generally, life was harsh and often short. Work was individually focused and concerned with doing whatever necessary to survive.

The second wave: agriculture. During this wave, people figured out that planting seeds meant it was possible to grow a food source and there was less (or no) need to be nomadic. This changed the world because there were many things to learn and adapt to, such as agriculture, common language, and how to barter and trade. The result was people created business, governance, and villages. Essentially, people from varying tribes or backgrounds had to learn to live with one another. The agriculture model lasted tens of thousands of years. In this wave, the model of work meant one person was expected to take on multiple roles and jobs. A farmer would never say, "That's not my job." Similarly, "doing it all" is still the same model today for many small business owners. Finally, in this wave, even though work was still independent, there was a community interdependence.

Then came the third wave: Industrial Revolution. In this model, work became segmented. If a person worked at an automobile factory, they did not make the whole car. Instead, they only assembled a small part of the car, i.e., wheels or doors, etc. The phrase "that's not my job" became common in this model of work. The Industrial Revolution began in the late 1700s for Europe and the early 1800s in the United States. The Industrial Revolution introduced the top-down model of operations, and while this model is only about 220 years old, the whole world seems to be organized by it. In this model, those at the top controlled everything, including decision-making, goal setting, work assignments, communications, finances, organization structure, etc. Those in the middle implemented what those at the top wanted, and those at the bottom of the chart (entry-level workforce) simply did what they were told and no more. The entry-level workforce was not required to think or problem solve and was often actively discouraged from doing so. The workforce did not see the big picture, was not engaged, and a job was just a job. In the early years, entry-level or line workers were considered a disposable resource since there were many others wanting work.

TOP-DOWN MODEL

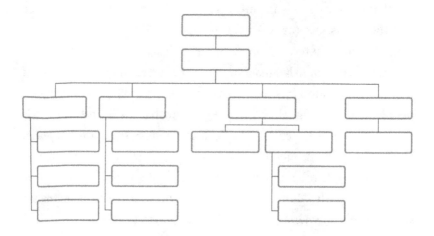

Could it be that the top-down model is one of the root causes of many of our problems? Could it be that the top-down model of leadership and organization is the root cause of many misaligned organizational policies, practices, and problems? Worse yet, organizations have accepted this model as the only one for over two hundred years. We have not seriously challenged how work is organized. Instead, we have spent over one hundred years trying to mitigate the negative impacts of this model beginning with Frederick Taylor's scientific management theory in 1911. We have tried efficiency studies, team building, motivation, employee benefits, self-directed work teams, quality circles, matrix organizations, servant leadership, inverted pyramid, customer-oriented cultures, strategic planning, and dozens of other programs and initiatives that attempt to improve performance. While all these programs certainly have made their contribution, none have fundamentally changed the way organizations are designed from the top down. One of the primary challenges with the top-down model is that work is divided up by functions, which encourages siloes.

What if organizations were designed differently and not by function? What if organizations were structured by mission or purpose, or relationships, or customers, or some other criteria? Would that eliminate many of the current problems caused by the top-down model or would there be a new set of corresponding problems? So much effort has been given to attempting to mitigate the negative impacts of the top-down model with marginal success, maybe it is the top-down model that needs to go. Maybe it is time to consider a more people-centric organizational structure. After all, an organization only exists as a name on a legal document: people are the organization. Maybe it is time organizations are designed around the people as opposed to stuffing people into an artificial structure. Consider the following what-ifs:

- Employees evaluate managers and the managers must reach a certain threshold of ratings or they can no longer be managers.

- There are only two to three levels in the entire organization.
- There are only two to three pay levels in the organization, and everyone in a level receives the same compensation.
- Customers evaluate employees.
- Each work team does its own hiring, firing, and disciplining.
- Managerial positions rotate periodically, and the new manager can undo what the previous manager implemented.
- Underperforming individuals are paid to leave the organization.
- Individual compensation is based 50 percent on individual contribution, 25 percent on team success, and 25 percent on total company success.
- There are no titles. Everyone is a contributor.
- There is no differential in any of the typical class artifacts like larger offices, being on mahogany row, corporate benefits, stock options, etc.
- Everyone has a mentor, and there are peer evaluations.
- Everyone genuinely cares for and supports one another.

The top-down model might well be the origin of the need for organization development in organizations. This is stating the obvious because before there were organizations, there would not have been a need for organization development. People in power in organizations do not necessarily want to relinquish that power to the employees for them to innovate, create, and design a work product or work environment to their liking. Those who rose to power did so by navigating the existing top-down model, so why change it? This model does not align with organization agility, the premise of which is that organizations need to have teams of individuals that can deploy to solve problems, nor does it align to the research on employee engagement that says employees want to broaden and build skillsets and move through job experiences that align to their interests. The negative effects of the top-down model continue to cause challenges for organizations, and an alert OD practitioner can help organizations move past the constraints and negative impacts of the top-down model.

WHERE DID OD START?

There are many different perspectives on the origins of organization development. Our perspective is that it emerged from the needs of organizations that were built during the Industrial Revolution. Listed here are a few of the more frequently identified origins.

- The origins of OD may have begun with the development of the Industrial Revolution. Before then, there were trades, shopkeepers, farms, and other organizations that were small, usually family-run operations. That all changed during the Industrial Revolution with the introduction of large industrial organizations. This led to large industrial complexes and the top-down model of management, the hierarchy, the division of labor, and social classes, i.e., laborers, foreman, management.

- Early organizational studies centered around increasing labor productivity. The accepted process for a foreman was to yell at and threaten laborers to motivate them. In his *Principles of Scientific Management* (1911), Frederick Taylor realized that the problem was not the workers, but the process. Thus, he found a way to make workers more productive not by yelling at them, but by changing the process. At Bethlehem Steel Company, Taylor concluded that the efficiency of the whole operation could be significantly improved if each man had the appropriate shovel based on the weight of the material they were shoveling. This may have been the beginning of an awareness that organizational processes affect performance.

• From 1927 to 1932, productivity studies at the Hawthorne plant (electric lighting) in Cicero, Illinois, produced what is known as the Hawthorne effect (Mayo, 1928; Landsberger, 1958): if people are paid attention to, their productivity tends to increase. This may have been the beginning of an awareness that relationships matter and how supervisors and managers interact with their employees matters. Some attribute the beginnings of OD to the Hawthorne studies. Kurt Lewin (1930) introduced us to social psychology and the action research method and was instrumental in founding National Training Labs NTL (1947).

• The 1940s brought *Theory of Human Motivation* (1943) from Abraham Maslow and further research into human motivation. The socio-technical system (STS) identified the organization as both a social system and a technical system. The 1950s brought the system thinkers with theories, including social, ecological, language, organizational, and management systems. The influence systems have on human behavior has strong roots during this period. Teambuilding became popular during this period as part of building the social system.

• The 1960s and 1970s brought a strong emphasis on testing, standards, and fairness. This was a period of disruption with the civil rights movement, diversity and inclusion issues, an unpopular Vietnam War, a decline in national productivity, and a shift from manufacturing to a customer service orientation. Douglas McGregor's work on Theory X and Y was prominent in the early 1960s. T groups (first articulated by J. L. Moreno, 1914–15), the Tavistock Institute (founded 1946), and Carl Rogers's humanistic psychology and self-actualization (1959), were all influential as well.

- The 1980s and 1990s brought changes in leadership styles and the leaders' increased awareness of their impact on the organization's culture. There was a growing awareness that the command-and-control top-down model may no longer be appropriate for the modern workforce, and there were many attempts at changing this approach: self-directed work teams, quality circles, matrix organizations, inverted pyramid, servant leadership, and others.

It is safe to say there are many different opinions and time frames on the origin of OD. Part of the difficulty in identifying a specific person, theory, or time frame is that OD as a field has evolved and continues to evolve to this day.

Some would say the constant evolutions are good, as it demonstrates the flexibility of the field to meet the needs of a changing environment, while others would say this inability to define the field and its attempt to include everyone and all activities hurts the field and confuses the population at large as well as practitioners in the field. Both positions have merit, and further time and investigation may ultimately determine the final impact/consequence.

ORGANIZATION DEVELOPMENT MODELS

A model is a visual representation designed to show the appearance of something. A model is someone's interpretation or characterization of reality. A model is a mental and visual construct and is not the actual object: just as a map is not the actual roads, the model is not the organization. Models can be useful in understanding the interconnectedness of the elements or in getting a big picture or a different perspective. There is no perfect model, and most, if not all, models have flaws, but nevertheless, some models are useful.

Three-dimensional models may do well in showing the big picture; however, organizational models are usually two dimensional which limits their ability to show the full picture. Still, they can show the various systems, core and supportive, and their connection to other elements of the organization. A core system is one that is vital to the organization, while a supportive system is more helpful than vital. All organizations have both, and both are necessary to successfully implement the mission and accomplish its goals. It is possible to have two similar organizations with different core systems depending on the strategic plan and goals of the organization. Even within the same industry, the same organizational model may not be appropriate for different organizations. One organization could be emphasizing growth, profitability, and shareholder value. In this organization, finance may be more dominant (core). In the competitor's organization, their strategy might be quality and customer service. In this organization, operations may play a more dominant role (core). If working with these two organizations, different models may or may not be warranted, but certainly, the emphasis on which elements of the model are more germane is.

There are models for organizational process and design. Each in turn will be addressed here. Organizational models provide a template that often guides organizational diagnosis. Additionally, they can and often do provide a pathway for improvement initiatives. Organizational process models tend to reflect their industry. There have been many manufacturing models: Six Sigma, just in time, lean manufacturing, Deming fourteen points, and statistical process control. These models are excellent for manufacturing but may not be as relevant to the banking industry or nonprofits. Other process models may be better suited for certain industries, and then there are those models that tend to be generic but may lack some of the intricate elements and sophistication of a more specific model.

Currently there are a number of different popular approaches (processes) to organizational improvement in the literature, including diagnostic (Beer & Spector, 1993; Cummings & Worley, 2009), dialogic (Bushe & Marshak, 2015), appreciative inquiry (Cooperrider & Whitney, 2001), and agile organizations (Anderson, 2019). Most of these models also assume an open system (Katz and Kahn, 1978) as there are few examples of closed systems that are not affected by their environment.

Naturally, each author advocates for their theory, which tends to encourage a singular or more myopic approach. All of these approaches have merit and application opportunities, and there is no reason for the OD practitioner to adopt just one approach. The reality is that the OD practitioner often uses whatever approach best fits the client as well as their own implementation style. There is no reason why a combination of these approaches cannot be used on any initiative.

In medicine, there is a model "Diagnosis before Prescription," and that model applies well to any organization development effort. To develop a plan of action, a strategy, or a vision, before knowing what the current situation is, what the goals are, or what the organization is attempting to improve, and what the system is currently supporting can be an expensive and resource consuming effort without sustainable change, a risky proposition. The diagnostic model provides many ancillary benefits, including but not limited to the following:

- An opportunity to build trust with the client.
- An opportunity to build your relationship with the client.
- Obtaining a solid view of their culture.
- Diagnosing their level of emotionality (discussed later in this book).
- Diagnosing their level of resistance.

- Uncovers other unknown problems.
- Begins the transfer of ownership of the problems and solutions.
- Identifies measurable objectives.
- Helps identify targeted areas for change.
- Sets a purpose for any change activities.

Given all these and many other benefits for using a diagnostic approach, it is hard to imagine an organizational change effort without gaining a thorough understanding of current conditions. A practitioner will benefit from being aware that diagnostic work is also inherently part of the intervention (Schein, 1998). As you are engaging with the client, there will be many opportunities to model behavior that will influence the organization members (use of self), and there will be opportunities to have discussions and influence change at many levels of the organization (from leadership to individual contributor). As mentioned in other areas of this book, the phases of OD are fluid and overlapping, and recognizing when there is overlap and how to adapt to the changing phases and opportunities is evidence of a skillful practitioner. It is also worth noting that in certain situations, such as in a crisis, moving immediately into a solution or short-term fix may be appropriate.

ORGANIZATION DESIGN

For this book, we reviewed over fifty different organizational design models and noted there was a high degree of similarity between many of them. The OD practitioner needs to be knowledgeable of the more generally accepted models that have withstood the test of time.

Knowing the different models, seeing where they interconnect and where they add a different or unique element, is important. Knowing the advantages and disadvantages of each model is also important. Being able to pick a model that will best fit, explain, or help an organization is essential. No one model fits all clients in all industries. At times, it may be necessary to take elements from several models to come up with the best model that will meet a client's needs and circumstances. Knowledge of many models will facilitate the OD practitioner being able to do this.

Also, other similar fields have their models as well. Change management has models such as John Kotter's eight step process from his book *Leading Change* (1995). Organization design has models, and there are many models of HR that provide a framework for analyzing human capital management. There are times when working with an organization these models may complement, overlap, or conflict with one another. The knowledgeable OD consultant can weave the important elements of each model and use what will help the client organization.

PROACTIVE VERSUS REACTIVE OD

Proactive OD is strategic in nature and involves anticipatory work done in advance of any overt problem or serious symptoms. Reactive OD is more of a cause-and-effect response, and it is usually done in reaction to some event or stimulus. Many OD projects are reactive when problems or symptoms occur and tend to be more focused on the amelioration of the problem. They also tend to have more of a singular focus than proactive OD initiatives. Because organizations may want help with a specific issue, the overwhelming majority of calls an external OD practitioner might receive will be reactive. Very few organizations initially hire anyone to change their culture or fix or improve their entire organization.

Reactive OD initiatives tend to be time-limited and singularly focused and because of those preexisting conditions tend to have more unintended consequences. Reactive OD initiatives frequently do not take the time to discern root cause and often treat the symptoms with limited sustained organizational benefits. They become "flavor of the month" programs much more frequently than proactive OD initiatives. Reactive OD initiatives, when beneficial, tend to benefit a smaller segment of the organization (a team, department, office, region), rather than the entire organization. Reactive OD initiatives tend not to be as systemic as proactive OD initiatives.

Instead, Proactive OD ties reviews or analysis to the goals, vision, or strategic plans of the organization, which encourages the OD practitioner to look at the entire organization systematically. This allows the practitioner to see the potential impacts on all other areas and departments of the organization. These initiatives are better able to eliminate many unintended consequences and ensure organizational sustainability.

How then does the OD practitioner turn a request for a simple reactive OD initiative into more of a proactive initiative?

- Through their understanding of organizational systems and the interconnection of all parts of the organization to one another.
- Knowing that a successfully implemented program in one department will affect everyone else that interacts with that department.
- Through discussion with those involved that will determine the impact on them as well as others.
- By helping senior leaders, or those requesting the initiative, to see the bigger picture or the potential fallout.
- By being constantly aware of potential unintended consequences and bringing them to the surface for discussion and resolution.

Turning a simple reactive request into a larger, deeper, more thorough look (proactive) at the issue may not always be welcomed. Ultimately, this may be easier for an internal OD practitioner than an external practitioner. An internal practitioner may have more organizational knowledge and see more of the connections than an external practitioner whose perspective is more limited.

FROM REACTIVE TO PROACTIVE

The initial client request was to help the internal dynamics of one team, in essence, to reduce their conflict and become more cooperative with one another. The practitioner suggested interviewing every member of the team, as well as key individuals from other teams who frequently interacted with the team. During the interviews, significant information regarding other parts of the organization was revealed. So much information was revealed during initial interviews that the practitioner recommended expanding the interview to additional members of the organization. Once all of the information was collected, it was presented to management who then realized that the problem was far greater than originally thought. Everyone in the room realized that proceeding with the original request was myopic and a waste of time and money. The result was a more significant intervention process expanding to the whole organization.

OD IN THE ORGANIZATION

In all too many organizations, the function of OD is placed within a department, most commonly human resources (HR) or training and development (T&D). Whatever department OD is attached to, it has the effect of minimizing the OD function and reducing its authority and credibility. The best location for OD is reporting to the highest organization level possible, typically the CEO or COO. OD needs to be able to support and help any part of the organization with authority and credibility. When OD reports to the CEO, then the practitioners speak with the voice of the CEO and department heads tend to listen better. This is especially important when strong silos exist within the organization or when the leadership style tends to be autocratic.

Our belief is that organization development is not part of training and development or human resources; rather, it is its own department and should have its own presence at executive meetings. The finance department might advise the CEO on mergers and acquisitions. The CIO might advise the CEO on the difference in their computing processes and hardware. Maintenance or engineering might advise the CEO on the age and quality of the physical structures, while operations might advise them on trucking distances and the like. The CHRO might advise the CEO on workforce planning and human capital issues. The OD department might advise the CEO on combining two organizational units with vastly different cultures or climates. The OD department might also advise the CEO on challenges related to culture and climate that are impacting productivity, turnover, or engagement.

Another reason to keep OD as a distinct department reporting to the CEO is that OD can then remain focused on OD work and not become diluted by taking on other responsibilities that belong elsewhere. OD would no doubt work closely with HR and T&D but may also work closely with other departments (i.e., finance, operations). OD then becomes a unifying force within the organization, encouraging collaboration and cooperation rather than advocating for its own department.

Any organizational change, no matter how small or large, then becomes the purview of OD. In today's constantly changing environment, OD practitioners will be quite busy with proactive system and work process reviews. Any time an organization can identify and resolve problems before implementing any changes, it can reduce unintended consequences and become more efficient and productive while reducing stress and negativity among staff.

INTERNAL VS. EXTERNAL PRACTITIONER

One question an OD practitioner or client may ask: "Is there a different set of skills needed by an internal *versus* external practitioner?" Many would argue yes, while others might argue that there is a core set of characteristics that apply to all practitioners regardless of where they practice (i.e., industry, organization, etc.). However, both are likely true. There are a core set of principles, skills, and knowledge all OD practitioners would benefit from having, and there are also job-specific skills and competencies a good OD practitioner would benefit from having.

Thus, the initial question is better framed as "Is it a different set of skills and competencies, or is it a different usage at a different time?" For instance, political awareness may be important to both the internal and external practitioner; however, the internal may already have considerable awareness due to their time in the organization, while the external may need to be more sensitive and alert to it during initial stages.

The organizational system might also influence the internal and external practitioner differently. Organizational history, systems, and processes likely influence the internal more so than an external. The familiarity with the system may make it more difficult for the internal practitioner to think objectively about the organization and its challenges. Additionally, job security, promotions, and acceptance may all have a greater effect/influence on the internal versus someone who is on a focused limited assignment as an external. These considerations are part of the reason there is considerable discussion on "use-of-self" in The Practitioner chapter.

Internal practitioners may need to be particularly sensitive to their position in the organization and who they report to. For example, the internal may be a part of an operational unit (e.g., human resources) which will have its own culture, rules, and processes, or they may sit in a part of the organization that allows for independence from any departmental influences. The internal practitioner may need to assess their ability, given their position, to influence the organization. For example, if the practitioner is in HR and is asked to lead an organization-wide change initiative, what level of support will other leaders inherently provide to HR? Will buy-in from leaders outside of HR be easily attainable, or is this an extra challenge because initiatives from HR are viewed as "check-the-box" or "flavor of the month"?

Another consideration is whether an internal practitioner can provide their reports or findings directly to the client or do their bosses within their department have to review and approve first? In which case, are the reports from their office truly unbiased or are they edited to do things such as avoid ruffling feathers?

Internal practitioners may face considerable challenges based on their position; however, the process of building relationships within the organization may favor the internal practitioner over external practitioners. Building positive interpersonal relationships is critical to both internal and external practitioners; however, internals may have a slight advantage in that they may be afforded more time, access, and availability given that they are an employee. An external practitioner may not be afforded the same time and access to people during an engagement which may result in greater challenges in forming and nurturing a productive partnership with the client.

Another considerable area of difference for internals and externals is exit strategies. Externals often have a plan for how and when they will leave an organization and may develop an internal infrastructure that can carry on the initiative or change independently. Internals may not have the same sense of urgency or the establishment of an internal infrastructure since they can provide ongoing support. Internals are a part of the system as well as a change agent, if an internal practitioner feels that the system is no longer capable of change or feels like the system is not one to remain a part of, then an internal practitioner may have to make the tough decision to exit the system or organization.

There are a lot of ways that internals and externals may have to navigate organizations and situations differently, sometimes using the same competencies. The discussion could extend beyond competencies into what kinds of personalities and values are better suited for a particular practitioner role. Extending the discussion to include researchers, scientists, academics, global and social specialists, and conflict resolution and change management consultants adds additional complexity. If we do, we may find there are different competencies and skills required for all those roles. However, if we focus on the OD practitioner (whether internal or external), there appears to be a core set of competencies that are germane across those roles.

INTERNAL AND EXTERNAL PRACTITIONER: WHAT IF YOU ARE BOTH?

An external OD practitioner might find themselves as an internal OD practitioner when it comes to their own organization. As an OD practitioner employed within a consulting organization, it is not necessarily easy to "turn off" the practitioner skill set when considering your employer organization dynamics. Just because an organization specializes in practicing OD for customers does not mean it is immune to the same challenges its clients face. As a result, an external practitioner may also have to focus their skills inward to the organization where they work.

When working internally with your employer, there are many factors to consider: political capital with leaders, relationships with colleagues, and personal morals and values driving engagement with the organization. Choosing which "battles" to pick to make meaningful change and how much of an influence you can have within a particular situation is also important. There are times where there is a clear right or wrong approach to take; however, there is often a time where the practitioner must decide which approach is acceptable, good, better, or best. In these instances, a practitioner will factor the uniqueness of their client situation and their capabilities as a practitioner to best support the situation. Each situation will require judgment and weighing options before taking (or not taking) action.

DISCUSSION QUESTIONS

The following questions are intended to be thought provoking and to encourage organizational or individual analysis and introspection.

Ideally, these questions are discussed in small groups; however, many questions can easily be undertaken for individual consideration.

- What is your organization's history and how does it impact you today?
- Do you have a top-down model and how does it affect the organization today?
- What is your, or your organization's understanding of organization development?
- Are you an internal or external practitioner? How does your role fit into client organization systems?
- Given your current clients, in what ways could you engage in proactive OD initiatives?
- What is leadership's expectation of you or your role in your organization?
- What might be encouraging competition rather than cooperation in the organization?
- Are there any nonproductive behaviors and what might be tolerating or supporting them?
- Overall, how would you characterize the relationships within the organization? What is the impact of these relationships on the organization?

CHAPTER THREE

About the Practitioner

INTRODUCTION

In OD, practitioners need to be acutely aware of self. This includes being aware of your values, biases, preferences, knowledge, skills, and competencies. It also includes knowing how to model behavior and reflect what the practitioner hopes leaders will model once work is finished and a partnership is ended. Being sensitive to the environment and in touch with your own emotions, reactions, and judgments become important in being an effective OD practitioner.

KNOWLEDGEABLE PRACTITIONER VS.
SKILLFUL PRACTITIONER

There are many ways a practitioner can gain knowledge in the field of OD. There are graduate programs that offer degrees in organization development, change management, organizational psychology, human resources, and other associated areas. Within these programs, there are often many different areas of focus: research, statistics, testing and measurements, system theory, etc. Most, if not all, programs provide a solid foundation and an extensive body of knowledge regarding their chosen area. As a result, graduates will have read about the history of OD, past and current theories of OD, competencies in OD, systems theory, behavioral change, and the future of OD. However, for many students, especially if they are not in the working world, the opportunity to effectively apply this knowledge in a timely fashion may be limited or lacking entirely. The application of this knowledge is where you transition from a knowledgeable practitioner to a skillful practitioner.

At some point, a practitioner is going to interact with people, and it is then, when knowledge, skills, and abilities are applied, that they become a skillfull practitioner. You can talk about all the elements involved in cultural change (a knowledgeable practitioner) or you can get immersed in discovering, diagnosing, and planning improvements for all of those same elements (a skillful practitioner). How skillful you are as a practitioner depends more on your experiences and confidence levels than any body of knowledge you might have. Intervening in a complex interconnected living ecosystem, being able to build trusting positive relationships with everyone at all levels within the organization, and being aware of your own biases and predilections are skills not often acquired during the safety of graduate school but more often in the high-stakes real world. To be clear, we are not saying one is more important than another; rather, both are important, and each has their place.

COMPETENCIES

As with all occupations, certain competencies are required to be successful. There have been many attempts by professional associations, practitioners, and academics to establish a set of core competencies for OD practitioners. Despite the many published articles, books, and opinion papers discussing OD competencies, there is still no universal set of agreed-upon competencies that describe OD practitioners. Furthermore, many competencies that appear in one model appear in another model under a slightly different name or in a different order.

We recognize that there is no standard set of competencies that the field uses as a benchmark. However, we also recognize that it does not seem appropriate to ignore this topic in a book trying to support an emerging OD practitioner. An OD practitioner will do well to understand their strengths, weaknesses, areas of competence, and areas for growth to progress through the field. Thus, some baseline understanding of competency for OD practitioners is necessary.

At a minimum, OD practitioners benefit from gaining expertise in the competencies listed below. These competencies are found across many competency models that exist for OD practitioners and are foundational to the practice. Each OD practitioner can continually assess performance in these areas and decide where to focus developmental efforts.

Core Competencies

- Relationship Management: The ability to develop positive trusting interpersonal relationships at all levels within the organization. Excellent communications skills.
- Situational Awareness: A sensitivity and consciousness of interpersonal, political, cultural, and environmental issues.
- Systems Thinking: A solid understanding of the influence of systems, policies, and work processes on human behavior.
- Assessment/Analysis: Good diagnostic skills, able to determine the root cause. The ability to differentiate symptoms, from systems, from solutions.
- Organization Development Theory: Strong knowledge base and grounded in one or more organizational models.
- Use of Self: Strong understanding of self, biases, values, and your personality and knows how to use self, strong ethics. Being a positive and motivating influence within the organization.

- Human Capital Management: Basic understanding of principles of human capital management.
- Decisiveness: The ability to decide and commit to an approach for a client situation.
- Problem-Solving: The ability to determine root cause and see beyond simple cause and effect and offer practical, timely, and cost-effective solutions to clients.

The goal here was not to identify every competency necessary for the practitioner to be successful, but to identify essential or core competencies and provide a reasonable definition of each. These will give any practitioner a good start and plenty to work on since few if any practitioners are consistently good at all of the above.

USE OF SELF

Use of self is a broad topic that can cover many different areas of self-awareness, so it is worth spending some extra time discussing in this book. Many fields discuss this concept, including social work, counseling, therapeutic interventions, nursing, hiring, and others. While there are many and sometimes ambiguous definitions of the use of self, the concept has wide acceptance. Essentially, the use of self refers to the awareness and sensitivity of yourself and being able to use that knowledge and integrate it into your professional work.

An OD practitioner may have an extensive body of knowledge, understand systems and processes, and may possess great facilitation skills; however, the use of all these tools depends very much on who they are, their values, personality, and use of self as an instrument of change. OD practitioners with advanced degrees, and possibly years of experience, who are not in touch with self, may end up doing more harm than good in an organization. In the use of self, the OD practitioner aims to exemplify the behaviors and attitudes they are advocating for the organization. The goal is to model the type and style of leadership they are encouraging within the organization. Otherwise, they risk being seen as duplicitous and a charlatan. The OD practitioner needs to be trustworthy as they will often be given confidential and personal information and organizational plans. Any violation of trust will render the OD practitioner ineffective as a change agent and facilitator. Missteps that reduce trust with a client are usually terminal for external OD practitioners and a major setback for internals.

The use of self (i.e., what you see, hear, touch, sense, smell, think, and feel) is an excellent barometer that provides clues to the organization's culture and processes. Chances are that if you feel or think a certain way or are affected in a certain way by the organization, so do others within the organization. The use of self as an organizational gauge or barometer is an important service any OD practitioner can provide. Time and time again employees will use the OD practitioner as a sounding board or vent their frustrations, and these are all clues to the organization's culture and process. The OD practitioner is always in a data-gathering mode regardless of the activity they are performing. Every piece of information can be considered a tile that goes into the mosaic even though it may not make sense until you step back and see the whole picture. The rule of thumb is that if you see it, hear it, sense it, feel it, then say it. Bring it out in the open for discussion. This raising of awareness of the issues and bringing them out into the open is a valuable service the OD practitioner provides. In this way, the OD practitioner is engaging in the use of self to navigate client situations.

The elephant in the room occurs when there are one or more big issues that employees know about, but they are never put on the table for discussion and resolution. Once again, the OD practitioner can be invaluable in situations like these by being willing to speak truth to power and to bring up these issues. Once they are out in the open, issues can usually be intelligently discussed and resolved. The OD practitioner can be invaluable in managing the emotions of the group as well by creating a safe environment for all. The focus is on the problem, not the people, and not blame. Identify the current situation and the future ideal situation and then focus on how to get from the current state to the desired state.

The following sections describe several concepts related to the use of self. These concepts are important to self-assess and embark on efforts to improve the use of self as a practitioner. Developing these areas is not a one-time effort. Rather, it is a continual activity to monitor and assess how you are doing in these areas.

SENSITIVITY TO SELF

As illustrated in the previous paragraphs, the OD practitioner is an instrument of change, and using your mind, emotions, and senses in that regard is important and a valuable service to the client. This means, however, that the OD practitioner needs to be highly sensitive to the environment and themselves *and* willing to bring up the difficult issues. Developing a sensitivity to your own emotions and those of others is a lengthy process for most individuals. Many individuals who could be described as "highly sensitive" have been to dozens of workshops, lectures, and seminars and read self-help and psychology books. They have often gone through coaching or therapy to gain a better understanding of their own upbringing and personality. The journey to understanding yourself is usually long and hard yet rewarding. Being a good OD practitioner is not simply having a good theoretical understanding. It is being able to use that information for the betterment of the people and organizations one serves. The use of self is critical in that endeavor, and to effectively engage in the use of self-concepts, you must first start by being in touch with yourself. The following ten areas are instrumental in getting in touch with self.

- Identify your core values.

  o One's values are often acquired unconsciously through upbringing, not conscious decision. This activity will require you to make conscious decisions about how you choose to live your life and what is important to you. Core values are those that you feel are essential to your life. It is a best practice to limit core values to six or less. The rule of thumb here is that the more values you have, the more likely you will violate one or more of the values and/or not remember your values.

- Understanding your personality type—MBTI or similar assessments.

  o Are you a "people" person or "task" focused? Type A personality (concept first described by Friedman and Rosenman, 1950) or laid back? Easy to get along with (i.e., tolerant, patient, flexible) or stricter and more judgmental? Chances are good that those you do not get along with have a different personality and set of values.

- Understanding your conflict resolution preferences— TKI or similar assessment

  o How competitive are you? How much do you compromise? How much do you accommodate others? How much do you avoid conflict? How much do you collaborate? Knowing how you deal with conflict and learning to become comfortable with conflict will allow you to better help your clients in this area.

- Knowing your biases or preferences.

  o   Merely accepting the fact that other people will have different biases and preferences allows you to be more tolerant of the differences you will undoubtedly encounter when you work with others.

- Being emotionally intelligent and competent.

  o   Given that most of us may not have received a lot of training in this area while growing up, it will require considerable effort as an adult to learn how to sense our own emotions and use them appropriately. This may well be a life-long journey. More about this is written later in this section of the book.

- Using your reactions as a diagnostic tool.

  o   You are an instrument of change, and merely by being present, you will affect the environment. Being sensitive to how you are reacting is a strong clue to how others are likely reacting as well. After all, there are only so many emotions human beings have, and there is a good chance if you feel a certain way, others do as well.

- Sensitivity and environmental awareness.

  o   Being aware of the atmosphere in the room or the company culture are clues to how people are behaving. Human behaviors produce the atmosphere. Your sensitivity to mood or individual or group temperament are all important clues to group dynamics.

- Culturally sensitive.

  ○ Being culturally sensitive is a sign of respect and intelligence. The practitioner will likely be accepted more easily if they are aware of and respect different cultures and their practices.

- Understanding your leadership/management style.

  ○ We all have a style, even if we are not yet aware of it and/or have a hard time describing it. How you interact with individuals affects your relationships with them. It is important to learn your predominant style and be flexible and adapt your style as appropriate.

- Presenting a positive attitude.

  ○ The brain seems to have an easier time dealing with negative thoughts than positive ones. This may have helped us survive (i.e., being suspicious and watchful) over the millennium, but today may not be as beneficial. Much more is written about this later in the book.

By no means is the above list meant to be complete or comprehensive, but it is a healthy beginning for anyone looking to be more aware of self and use that awareness in the service of others.

BECOMING SENSITIVE AS A FORM OF INTROSPECTION

According to data in an Infographic from Wyzowl (Wyzowl.com, July 5, 2017), the average attention span has shrunk by almost 25 percent in fifteen years. In 2000, the average attention span was twelve seconds, and in 2015, it was eight and one quarter seconds. An article by the *Telegraph* newspaper (February 11, 2011) said that we are receiving so much data that it is the equivalent of reading 174 newspapers every day. Given our daily exposure to millions of bits of information and the time and energy to process all that information, and how busy we all are mentally and physically, it is no wonder that we have a difficult time being mindful and paying attention to our thoughts, emotions, behaviors, and relationships. Taking the time to get in touch with oneself (being self-aware or mindful) is not high on most folks' daily to-do list. Being sensitive to how you are in relationship to the environment and being sensitive to your own and other's emotions usually take a back seat to current conscious stimuli and task management. Even environmental awareness is diminished when the brain is bombarded by high levels of stimuli. There are numerous assessments and surveys in the marketplace that help raise awareness of biases you may have. Additionally, a great way to learn about your own biases is to listen to your comments, your jokes, your manner of speaking, what you laugh at, how you judge others, what your dislikes and preferences are. Observe how people respond to you. These are all clues to how we think and behave. Be introspective and you will learn a lot about yourself.

POSITIVE ATTITUDE/DISPOSITION

It is a part of the OD practitioner's job to be a ray of light and a beacon of hope in an organization, to believe that organizations can and do change, to believe that change is necessary if an organization is going to evolve with the times and be relevant in the future. So, for OD practitioners, how you show up matters. If you have a negative disposition, are generally pessimistic, critical, cynical, or negative, you will likely experience challenges in many areas, including building trustworthy relationships, being credible, being accepted, and being an effective change agent. Your awareness of your disposition will be a critical skill in using oneself during client engagements.

Many times, you will be asked to help an organization that has a negative climate or has employees that are pessimistic about change and have a generally negative attitude about the organization. Neuroscience tells us that the brain has a negative bias and that, in earlier times, has helped keep us watchful and alive. When we meet a negative or pessimistic person, then this signifies a danger to our brain, which makes us cautious and less trustful of people. Thus, when we meet a positive or optimistic person, our brain generally does not engage in the fear response, which provides an opportunity for a positive outcome. We have never seen an effective negative OD practitioner. What is needed in any organizational change initiative is a combination of optimistic, realistic, and skeptical individuals that are willing to work toward improving their organization. There needs to be hope and optimism, not fear and pessimism.

In many ways, the success of any organizational change initiative depends on the OD practitioner. Being knowledgeable, personable, sensitive, aware, circumspect, detailed, strong, tenacious, compassionate, respectful, candid, honest, and caring will certainly lead to more successful change initiatives than the opposite. Who you are, how you show up, what you do, and how you relate to others matters. You are affecting the system just by being there, so be deliberate and thoughtful about your presence. Know who you are and how you influence others.

Highly negative people do not see themselves as negative but instead often think of themselves as practical, realistic, or being able to see problems that others do not see. Also, since being negative is their "normal," when they are negative, they think nothing of it; they do not even see it or hear it. They often do not realize the impact they are having on those around them or within the organization. It is an unconscious habitual way of thinking and behaving and a very difficult habit to break.

Does the culture influence the individual or does the individual make the culture? Yes, for both. It is quite common to find negative teams or groups within an otherwise positive organization as well as finding positive individuals within an otherwise negative team, although that circumstance seems to be a bit more difficult to maintain long term. So, what is the critical difference? Many times, it is leadership, and sometimes it is the nature of a particular team's work (system). It is easy to understand why certain individuals within an organization become negative or jaded. If they have been through "flavor of the month" projects that have cost significant effort for little to no sustainable changes or results, then it is reasonable that they might be skeptical about any future efforts. The OD practitioner will likely encounter one of three reactions to any change process.

1. Optimistic—Enthusiastic, positive individuals, filled with hope and eager to jump into the process.
2. Skeptical—Hopeful but doubtful individuals who often prefer to wait and see.
3. Cynical—Doubtful, judgmental, and vocal individuals that either consciously or unconsciously work to prove that this initiative will fail like all the rest.

Optimists tend to be eager to get going and may miss the difficulties involved in the change process. They are typically highly supportive, positive, and vocal. Skeptics range from severe to mild and tend to see at least some of the difficulties that lie ahead, while cynics tend to be highly negative, destructive, and undermine the process.

It is important to support both the optimist (to help others and to encourage) and the skeptics (to continue to be watchful for problems the initiative will likely encounter). Encourage the skeptics to work with the changes and watch for unintended consequences. Ask the cynics to stop being a negative or destructive force within the organization. Encourage the cynics to be aware of their attitude and beliefs and their impact on the organization and if they feel they cannot change their attitude to get off of the team and move on. Cynics are a powerful and destructive impediment to change.

Changing all of the subtleties of a culture from negative to positive is not easy, and it can wear everyone down, including the

OD consultant, and hurt all that they do. Additionally, changing a negative culture often takes a considerable amount of effort and time. To be constantly vigilant of the mood, atmosphere, language, and nonverbal clues that hurt the organization from moving forward. Negative people tend to focus on the past, which is history, and no one can do anything to change it, while positive people tend to have a future focus. That is where everyone's energy needs to be.

BROADEN AND BUILD THEORY

In 2009, Barbra Fredrickson published *Positivity: Top-Notch Research Reveals the 3-to-1 Ratio That Will Change Your Life*, which discussed her broaden and build theory (the role of positive emotions in positive psychology), wherein she stated that positive emotions allow the individual to be less defensive and open to more information, resources, creativity, etc., and the more open we are, the more positive we tend to be. It is a bit of an upward spiral just as negative emotions can cause us to be in a downward spiral. The long-term benefit of such positive emotions is feeling greater genuine positivity in everyday life. We posit that the same is true for organizations, that the more positive everyone in the organization is, the more positive the climate and culture and the more engaged the workforce. Positive emotions help to create a positive culture, which creates a great place to work.

Turning an organization from a negative, critical, and complaining culture to a positive culture is no easy task and is usually a long-term proposition. Do you change the individual behaviors or the system influences first? The answer is you change them all but start wherever the greatest leverage will be.

EMOTIONAL COMPETENCY

The OD practitioner would benefit greatly from having both emotional intelligence (EI) and emotional competence (EC). It is important to understand the difference between EI and EC. EI is being aware of your own emotions and sensitive to those of others. EC is the use of your own emotions as a source of information and as a motivator to action. Both are important. Generally, awareness (EI) comes before action or use (EC).

In 1990, Drs. Peter Salovey and John Mayer coined the term emotional intelligence and defined it. In 1995, Daniel Goleman published his book *Emotional Intelligence* and popularized the concept. He expanded on the work of Salovey and Mayer. The four main areas of EI are as follows:

- Self-Awareness: The ability to know your own emotions.
- Self-Management: The ability to manage those emotions appropriately.
- Awareness of Others: Sensitivity to the environment and others.
- Relationship Management: Using emotions to improve relationships.

In the Goleman model, awareness of self and others may be considered the EI part, and the management of self and other the EC part.

Another field, social perception, aligns nicely as well. Social perception is a field of study that focuses on both self-awareness and awareness of others and the environment, how we form impressions or make judgments based on perceived clues. Social knowledge, which is one's awareness of social norms and rules, helps to create our social norms and interactions with others and be aware of other people's emotions by picking up on both the verbal and nonverbal clues.

Daniel Goleman's work on emotional intelligence made it acceptable to discuss emotions in the workplace. It brought to light the importance of emotions in such areas as decision-making, critical thinking, behavioral impulses, and building relationships, among others. Before, people were told to leave their emotions at home; suddenly they were now told to bring their passion, joy, and creativity to work. Concepts such as passionate employees, positive relationships, creative workplaces, and employee engagement may well have roots in the sudden change of emotional acceptability.

Suddenly, emotional intelligence workshops sprung up across the world, sometimes without much regard to cultural differences. Having emotions, expressing emotions, or acting on emotions differ significantly in cultures around the world. For instance, historically in the US, if a man exhibits gentleness, compassion, cries, or is scared, he was labeled as weak, and if a woman showed anger or was aggressive, she was labeled differently and usually negatively. That cultural expectation, to a smaller extent, still exists in the US today. Whereas in another culture, a strong assertive woman might be expected and a man who can show his emotions might be the norm.

There is a big difference between teaching emotional intelligence and being emotionally intelligent or competent. You cannot have an intellectual discourse about your emotional life and expect to be more emotionally mature. That is akin to reading books on bodybuilding and expecting a better body. At some point, you must go to the gym if you want a better body. Concerning your emotional competence, at some point, you have to experience yourself emotionally and learn to use your emotions appropriately in the heat of the moment.

Emotions are the primary basis for all relationships. You like someone, feel safe with them, trust them, etc. Even if there is an intellectual attraction, the attraction is the emotional part. We usually do not say we like the person because there is an intellectual similarity, and even if we did, "like" is the emotional part. Happiness, joy, fun, love are all part of our emotional lives and the reason we get married, have lifelong partners, raise families, etc. Caring, compassion, helping others, passion are all reasons why we work and attempt to make a positive difference in life. Emotions give meaning to life.

Becoming emotionally competent is a process and not a training event. It begins as Goldman suggests, with your own emotional awareness. A sensitive OD practitioner is aware of their emotions and uses them in the service of their organization/client. They can sense moods, atmosphere, group dynamics, and use that information both diagnostically and during the implementation of improvements. They are further able to help the clients become sensitive to their own emotions and how they are affecting decision-making, communications, conflict, relationships, etc. Human emotions affect the working atmosphere, climate, and culture of the organization; in fact, it is safe to say that emotions affect all areas of our lives. Therefore, being aware of your own emotions and using them for the betterment of everyone around you becomes a critically important skill for everyone.

Unfortunately, we have seen all too often where the OD practitioner gets caught up with the issues or misses issues, because of becoming acculturated to the organization and accepting as normal obviously dysfunctional behaviors. They themselves become negative or critical verbally and become angry, frustrated, hurt, or sad, emotionally never realizing that these personal reactions are all significant and clues to the problems within the organization. Having emotional competency is critically important for the OD practitioner.

A STUDY IN EI [1]

How many words do you typically use to describe your own emotions? The greater your vocabulary, the easier it is for you to describe what you are experiencing. In classes all across the country, when adult participants were asked to place on a continuum, from light to intense, words that describe the four basic emotions (mad, sad, glad, scared),

---

[1] For approximately five years, Dr. Kokkelenberg taught an emotional competence class to thousands of individuals both in public and in-house seminars.

most could only place four to six words per emotion. However, in a group setting, they often generated ten to twelve words. A richness of vocabulary allows for increased awareness and sensitivity to one's own emotions.

Further, when the participants were asked at what level of intensity (unaware–strongly intense) they became aware of their emotions, many participants indicated levels one through three. However, when asked what they were feeling currently, most could not identify any emotions. Some insisted that they were not feeling anything, but the very act of "insisting" said otherwise. Our surveys concluded that most people are not aware of their emotions when they present themselves in a level one through three.

Emotional Awareness Chart[2]

1	Unaware
2	Vague Sense
3	Barely Noticeable
4	Intermittent Awareness
5	More Noticeable
6	Consciously Aware
7	More Dominant
8	Strong Consciousness
9	Intense Feelings
10	Emotions Dominating

Most of us are so busy cognitively (task-focused not self-focused) that our cognitive areas of the brain are dominating and blocking our emotional awareness. Those individuals that practice mindfulness, which is being aware of your thoughts, emotions, physical sensations,

---

2   Lawrence Kokkelenberg emotional competency program

and environment in a nonjudgmental manner, tend to live in the present and not the past or future. These individuals may be aware of their emotions at level one to three, but for most of us, our awareness comes in at level four to six, but even then, many people push these emotions aside for task accomplishment. That is why some people have frequent headaches or muscle stress areas at the end of the day. Their emotions have built up to the point where they are affecting their physiology.

That leaves many individuals not aware of their emotions until they become intense and intrude on our consciousness, level seven to ten. At this level of intensity, the emotions can no longer be ignored. The exception is happy–glad, which we probably laugh or smile at a much lighter level of intensity, although happiness can be covered up as well.

Emotions are a rich source of information that often is not obtained through logic or cognitive processes. The earlier the practitioner can get in touch with those emotions, the earlier the practitioner can use those emotions in the service of their clients.

ARE SOME EMOTIONS BETTER THAN OTHERS?

There are authors that classify emotions as "good and bad," "open or closed," even "right or wrong" emotions. This separation of emotions into good and bad categories is a harmful categorization. That is akin to saying that your arms are good but your legs are bad. All our body parts have a purpose as well as all our emotions. If certain emotions were not useful, then do you not think that by now evolution would have culled them from our system? This good and bad concept may have originated in physiology or cultural acceptability.

Neuroscience tells us that prolonged exposure to cortisol, which is released with anger, can cause brain cells to die even though short-term exposure to cortisol can motivate the individual. We also know that people who are under stress a lot have more physical ailments. Positive psychology tells us that genuinely happy people tend to get sick less and live longer with many fewer problems. It is the prolonged exposure to the emotion that affects the physiology, either good or bad, not so much the short-term exposure.

All our emotions are useful and serve critically important purposes. Emotions are a great source of motivation and are a quicker source of information than cognition. Emotions motivate us to action far more strongly than reason or cognition. Additionally, your emotions can help you sense the environment (danger) far more quickly than reasoning or intellectual processing. Have you ever been to someplace and said to yourself or others, "This does not feel like a safe place," and yet there was nothing you could point to that gave you that information? That is emotional awareness of your environment, not intellectual awareness. Later, you might notice the bars on windows, or barbed-wire fences, or security cameras. Emotions inform us much quicker and in ways the intellect cannot. Many, and maybe most, purchasing decisions are based on emotions, and then we rationalize/justify the decision with facts/information that supports our decision. You may buy a new car because you like it but say you bought it for the mileage or carrying capacity. Emotions give you a strong indicator on how you are reacting to the environment/relationship and can be used as valuable information in any diagnostic capacity.

JUDGMENTS

A judgment is the forming of an opinion, estimate, notion, or conclusion from circumstances presented to the mind. Every day we make thousands of judgments regarding our environment, people, and situations. Judgments help us categorize information and make sense of the world, and they are also limiting. Judgments help us maintain our safety. Think about all of the judgments you make while crossing a street or driving a car. On the other hand, we make assumptions and judgments about people or situations that do not involve our safety. When we make judgments, we tend to limit our ability to think of alternative options which can reduce creativity. Once we make a judgment about someone or categorize something, we are not as open to contrary information or opinions. Additionally, after a judgment is made, confirmation bias tends to set in, and we look for those behaviors or situations that confirm our previous judgment. When we make a judgment, we believe we have an answer and stop searching for alternatives or additional information.

From a neuroscience perspective, the brain, to conserve energy, tends to habituate as much as it can. Judgments serve that purpose. Once we make a judgment, we no longer have to expend any energy in future assessments. Once we say that person is a "............" (insert whatever word we use categorizes that person), we sometimes make that same judgment for our entire life. Once we have that person categorized, we no longer need to expend any future energy trying to figure that person out (the paradigm is formed), and we can move on to the next person.

Breaking the paradigm and letting new information in takes even more energy than forming the original opinion. This is because when we continue to think of that person as a "........." we constantly reinforce that belief and strengthen the axons of the neurons we are using to make that assessment. The more we call that person the word we are using, the stronger the thinking pattern that develops. So if you think of a person as a clown, it takes considerable energy to see that person as an intelligent, caring individual. As an OD practitioner, it is beneficial to have the knowledge that your view of the world, your paradigm, is your perception, and others will have a different paradigm and perception. Being able to accommodate different opinions, to understand both sides of an argument, is a sign of intellectual and emotional maturity, which are important skills for OD practitioners. This maturity will require a degree of self-confidence and humbleness at the same time. Maintaining an understanding of your judgments and paradigms and being willing to challenge them as you engage in OD activities will be a beneficial skill when working with all manners of clients. Reducing judgmental thoughts and behaviors and increasing curiosity has many benefits.

VALUES

We are often unaware of our values, so we do not necessarily attribute our behaviors to them. Sometimes our own behaviors violate our stated values (cognitive dissonance), and when that occurs, we often experience anxiety, which causes us to rationalize the behavior to reduce the anxiety. How do you react when your values are violated by others? If you value timeliness and people are often late, or value honesty and people often lie, how do you react? How do you judge them?

Because of the unconscious way our values influence us, it is useful to engage in an introspective process that identifies and names our values. There are many free tools to assist with this, such as the VIA Inventory of Strengths Survey (VIA-IS) (Peterson & Park, 2004; Peterson & Seligman 2004). Whether you use a free tool to guide the process or not, the introspection process will involve reflecting on your own values, how you were raised, and the values you hold today, to see how your values and behaviors might be affecting your perspective and work.

Your values and your understanding of them will determine how you engage with clients and how you want to influence client organizations. In organizations, there are both stated and real organizational values. The stated values are often posted on various walls throughout the organization and in annual reports. The real values are how people (i.e., employees in the organization) treat each other. It is not uncommon for the stated values to be violated and for the organization to fail to live up to those stated values. This is another great opportunity for the OD practitioner to affect the culture of the organization. Organizational values guide the behavior of employees, especially when those values are constantly reinforced.

INDIVIDUAL VALUES

From day one, children are encouraged to behave in certain ways and unconsciously become acculturated to the environment in which they are raised. The values that the parents or household have get transmitted to the children. Children then grow up with a set of values that they never consciously determine for themselves. In fact, in teaching Steven Covey's *The 7 Habits of Highly Effective People* (2004) curriculum all across the country with thousands of participants, when asked how many people consciously determined what their values were, very few individuals ever raised their hands. The OD practitioner would do well to consciously decide on and identify their values, to review what values they were raised with and assess if they are still valid today.

INTROSPECTIVE VALUES EXERCISE

The following is a simple introspective, yet powerful, exercise that will help the OD practitioner raise their consciousness about their values. In a quiet space and when you have at least sixty minutes, answer the following questions in writing.

1. What values were you raised with? Identify at least five. They could be around timeliness, respect, honesty, communications, etc. Are those values still valid for you today or do they need to be modified?
2. What additional values do you think are important for you to live by?
3. Develop a list of no more than six core values for yourself. Values tend to be one word i.e., honesty, respect, loving, etc.
4. In what areas of your life do you tend to violate your values, i.e., traffic stops and honesty?

Once you have identified your core values, for the first few months, check weekly to see where you might have violated any of your values or where you lived by the values. This weekly review will help keep you conscious of your values and encourage behavioral compliance. After *three* months, a minimum of a monthly review will help you stay conscious of your values all year. Living by your values in the small things of life helps you live by your values when a lot is on the line. Becoming a value-driven person is like exercising any other muscle. The more we exercise it, the stronger it gets.

VALUES VIOLATION

Are your stated values really your values, or do you just say they are your values? Many individuals violate their values more frequently than they think they do. This is an example of cognitive dissonance, when your stated words or values do not match your deeds. When this occurs, we often rationalize our behaviors rather than admit that on this occasion we did not live up to our own values. For example, you say you believe in honesty and then get pulled over for a minor traffic violation and you can get out of a $100.00 fine by telling a little lie. Then you justify lying by saying that everyone does this sort of thing. That is a whole lot easier than saying, "I was a dishonest person and lied to the police officer." Another frequent violation of values is people who say they are respectful and then talk poorly about others behind their back, or use foul language, or are dismissive of others, never realizing that they are not being respectful, but rude and/or disrespectful.

SLIPPERY SLOPE

The concept of a slippery slope as best as can be determined originated around 1985-90. It is an expression that alludes to sliding down a slick hillside, indicating the further down you go, the harder it is to get back up. It is a concept that is often used in law enforcement and ethics training programs. Often, people live their lives between a small range of acceptable behaviors identified by the solid lines with occasional incidents both above and below the dotted line. When your behavior falls below your stated values, your rationalizations increase to rid yourself of the cognitive dissonance. The slippery slope is both subtle and insidious.

How would your behavior change if you made a sincere effort to live within the solid lines? Do you think this would be difficult or easy for you? To behave with absolutely no embarrassing, unprofessional, or illegal behaviors would be difficult for most people.

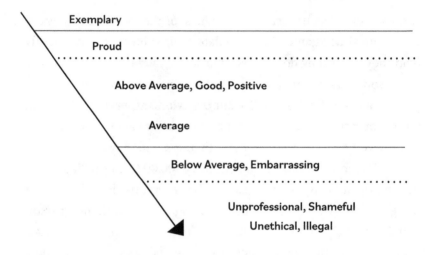

Developed by Lawrence Kokkelenberg Ph.D. All rights reserved.

SLIPPERY SLOPE CASE EXAMPLE

Restaurateurs like police offers in uniform in their establishments and will often give them a reduced meal price to attract them, and it is a way of saying thank you. Most police departments have rules against accepting freebie or reduced-price meals. They recognize it as a slippery slope.

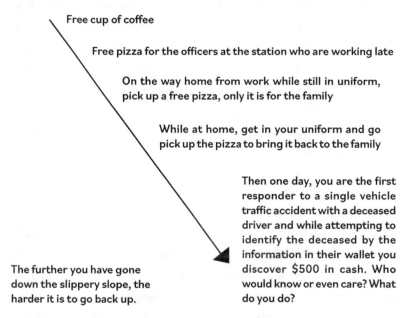

Free cup of coffee

Free pizza for the officers at the station who are working late

On the way home from work while still in uniform, pick up a free pizza, only it is for the family

While at home, get in your uniform and go pick up the pizza to bring it back to the family

Then one day, you are the first responder to a single vehicle traffic accident with a deceased driver and while attempting to identify the deceased by the information in their wallet you discover $500 in cash. Who would know or even care? What do you do?

The further you have gone down the slippery slope, the harder it is to go back up.

EMOTIONS AND VALUES

Living by your values may well depend on your emotional state at the time of an incident. If one likes another person, they probably will live more by their values than if they do not like them. For example, take the value of honesty. If a person (A) is walking ten steps behind another person (B) and sees person (B) reach into their back pocket and pull out a handkerchief and along with the handkerchief falls a twenty-dollar bill, they may well call out, telling them they dropped the twenty-dollar bill. Of course, they (Person A) could also rationalize and say that they were not 100 percent sure it fell out of their pocket and say it was their lucky day and pick up and keep the twenty dollars, in which case they may not be living up to their value of honesty. But that is very different than if the first person just took the parking space you were waiting for and now are angry and the same incident happened. Now one might see the twenty-dollar bill falling and know that they are going to have a free lunch with great joy and yet if you asked them what their values were, honesty would frequently be among them. This is a case where the individual's emotions influenced their behavior over their values, and further, they feel totally justified. The emotions the individual is experiencing influences whether they behave in accordance with their stated values or not. If an individual frequently steps over the line or violates their own values, then is it really their value or an aspiration?

BIAS

Dictionary.com (accessed July 17, 2021) defines bias as "a particular tendency, trend, inclination, feeling, or opinion, especially one that is preconceived or unreasoned." This definition covers both positive and negative bias. Often, when we say someone is biased, we tend to think about and see that person in a negative manner. We assume negative bias, yet we have both positive and negative biases. We often seek to reduce bias or be unbiased in many things we do, but the reality is all human beings are naturally biased. There is no such thing as an unbiased person. As a young child, we become biased toward learning one language, liking certain kinds of foods, climate, and cultural expectations. We call this upbringing, acclimatizing, or acculturating.

There is a fine line between a bias toward something and a habit. We have habits of how we think, emote, behave, and interact, and you could also say that we have a bias toward those processes or behaviors. Neuroscience tells us that the brain, to conserve oxygen and glucose, wants to habituate as much as possible to make it automatic without the expenditure of much energy. These habits, which all humans have, then become our biases. That is why there is no such thing as an unbiased person. Many biases are often based on stereotypes, or previous uninformed judgments and opinions, or peer or societal pressure, rather than facts or personal knowledge of an individual or circumstance.

We have many positive biases, such as getting exercise, eating healthy food, and moderation in alcohol, that enable us to live a healthy lifestyle. We may also have many other biases, most of which are unconscious, judgmental biases toward gender, sexual preference, age, ethnicity, country, religion, politics, and many other areas, which are often perceived as a negative bias.

Bias influences the work we do in organizations. For example, an area of concern is artificial intelligence since the programmers who are developing the algorithms may be inadvertently inserting their own biases. Machine learning is dependent on the quality of the learning templates just like human learning is dependent on the initial programming. Machines typically do not have bias, but their programs may. Machines operate on facts and logic, but human bias exists in machine learning from the creation of an algorithm to the interpretation of data and even the use of the data. Since many of our biases are unconscious biases, are programmers unconsciously programming machines to have their own biases?

Being aware of your own biases will enhance the OD practitioner's ability to adjust and change their behavior or thinking when their biases emerge, as they almost always do.

LEVELS OF BIAS AND PROBABILITY OF CHANGE

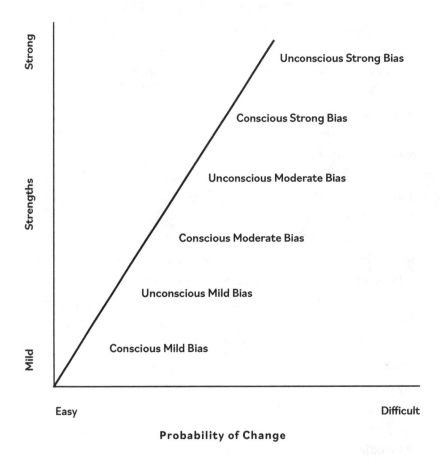

Probability of Change

Unconscious strong bias: The individual is both strongly biased and unaware, so there is little motivation to change as they believe there is nothing wrong with the way they think or behave. It is just the way they are or who they are. They may offend other individuals, but either are unaware or do not care. They are likely to be highly judgmental and opinionated. These are individuals who may not always be right, but they are never in doubt. The problem is others, never themselves. They may be quick to blame and often do not take responsibility for their own actions. Unless there is a major crisis in their lives, change will not be easy.

Conscious strong bias: The individual has strong biases but is aware of at least some of those biases and can voice their awareness of the same. They have reasons (justifications or experiences) for those biases. They may intend to say what they do and not care about the impact. They may be verbally derogatory of a person, gender, group, or class of individuals. If made aware, they may be more open to feedback about the harmful effects of their behavior.

Unconscious moderate bias: Generally these individuals are not as offensive as those with strong biases; however, their unawareness makes them less sensitive and motivated to make any changes. Offensive behaviors such as jokes, slang names, and derogatory comments are common and usually not intended.

Conscious moderate bias: Usually there is a decent level of awareness of some of their biases, which they may call preferences, as well as some level of unawareness. They may be open to feedback, and if the realization of the hurtfulness of their comments or behaviors is brought to their attention, they may be motivated to change.

Unconscious slight bias: This involves just about everyone, and in general these minor biases are not as hurtful nor as frequent. They involve off-color jokes, racist or sexist slurs, ways of thinking about a group or person, assumptions, and judgments.

Conscious slight bias: Preferences or previously concluded points of view that individuals hold about others or the world around them. They are aware of their beliefs but do not tend to see them as biases. They respond well to new factual data.

You can call them preferences, interests, or biases, and we all have many of them from the clothes we wear, the food we like, the things we do, and the way we think.

Conscious bias is more easily managed, and unconscious bias tends to affect us unknowingly and is often unmanaged until after it is out in the open, such as a sexist or racist joke or seemingly innocent ethnic name.

WHAT ARE MY PREFERENCES?

The OD practitioner would do well to consider scaling work to their abilities. What is your passion? What are your strengths? What are those elements you would prefer not to do or are not good at? Where do you want to focus your energy? What is your current family life circumstances, etc.? All of these kinds of questions provide information to consider when choosing your clients and focus at work. Here is a sampling of those introspective questions that one might ask oneself.

- Would you rather be your own boss, or would you rather have one or more bosses?
- Would you rather be an internal OD employee or external OD consultant?
- How much travel do you want to do? Some, none, or frequent? International as well as local?
- What family obligations do you have?
- Do you like working with mega organizations with over 100,000 employees worldwide, with many different cultures and complex interconnected systems, or do you like mom-and-pop organizations (less than fifty people) that are smaller and have less formal policies, and are more flexible?
- What level of responsibility are you comfortable with? Do you want complete project responsibility, or do you prefer to only focus on one area at a time?
- What are your own financial goals, and can you reach them more quickly by having a steady paycheck (internal) or by growing your own business (external)?

- Do you want to focus on a particular type of industry or market segment or do you want to be more of a generalist and take on all clients/industries?
- What phase of organization development are you best at: diagnostics, design, development, or delivery?
- How much work do you want? Do you want work-life balance or is working sixty hours a week okay with you? Can you get that free time better by being an internal or external?
- How good are you at working with and building positive trusting relationships with strangers? Externals may have more of a need to do this than internals.
- Do you want to build and manage your own business? Do you like supervising and mentoring others?
- How big do you want to grow and what is the best way to do that?
- How important is variety to you? Where can you best get that variety (internal/external)?

No OD practitioner is good at everything, so focusing on your strengths and preferences may be important for career success. Additionally, clients will often ask a practitioner if they can do certain activities to support the organization (such as deliver a class or coach an executive); you want to be able to confidently say yes or no to these requests. In cases where you need to say no, you will likely want to be able to refer a client to a competent professional; therefore, you may find it is important to build a network of individuals that have skills and abilities in the areas you do not. This network can help supplement your work with clients and provide expertise and support during a client engagement that you may otherwise not have been able to provide.

CONCLUSION

The concepts presented in this chapter are intended to help a practitioner see the value in introspection and understanding the critical nature of the use of self in OD. The practitioner is a tool in the process, just like OD models, theories, and assessments. There is significant value in recognizing the impact a practitioner has on the OD process and subsequently engaging in continuous self-assessments for purposes of growth and improvement.

DISCUSSION QUESTIONS

- In what ways do you use yourself as a barometer?
- Does your organization have more of a positive or negative atmosphere? What contributes to that?
- What are your personal stated and real values?
  - How do these compare to the stated and real values of your organization?
- Do the organization's values or your personal values guide your behavior?
- What were some examples when you have gone down on the slippery slope?
- What are judgments you have made that guide your assumptions and perceptions of others?
- What are your biases?
- How resistant to change are you?
  - How resistant to change is your organization?
- Which people in your organization tend to be "quick to judge"? How do you counter that?

CHAPTER FOUR

About the Organization

INTRODUCTION

Now that chapter three has discussed the OD practitioner in depth, the focus shifts here to talking about organizations and their characteristics or aspects that a practitioner may want to be aware of during any diagnostic and intervention. Each organization is unique in many aspects of its design, such as its mission, vision, values, climate, and culture; these are broad characteristics that a practitioner may want to consider when engaging with a customer. This chapter discusses design characteristics and other aspects of organizations, such as emotionality and values.

WHAT IS AN ORGANIZATION?

One definition of an organization is "an organized collection of people with a specific purpose, including business, government, association, even society" (adapted from Dictionary.com, 2021). It is reasonable to say that OD may happen in three main categories of organizations: government (public), corporate (private), or not-for-profit. These three kinds of organizations are inherently different. Government organizations certainly have a lot less control over the mission and purpose as those are usually prescribed by law. Not-for-profit organizations will generally have a strong sense of purpose as their existence is driven by a particular humanitarian, community, or similar need. Finally, corporations have a lot more variety in both mission and purpose, but also size, structure, outputs, etc. Practitioners may choose to focus on a particular category (i.e., government) of organizations or may go so far as to specialize in certain kinds of corporations (i.e., women-owned, small family business, Fortune 500, etc.). This decision is up to each practitioner and may change over time. OD can help improve any organization, regardless of its structure, processes, and practices.

DEFINING ORGANIZATION DESIGN

While there is a need to consider culture, climate, and behaviors as a part of organization design, it is important to distinguish design from organization development. So what is the distinction? Organization design focuses on creating structures, jobs, talent management practices, performance management programs, and general business processes that lead to organization performance. The design of an organization focuses on aligning the structure and processes to the organization's purpose and mission.

Design is often assumed to be solely about structure, putting boxes on paper, and aligning the hierarchy. While this is part of design, it is not the whole story. Design of organization structure involves determining the kinds of work units required to execute the work and then defining those work units with a functional statement. The function of each work unit will determine the kinds of jobs required to execute the function. For example, a common work unit is "finance," which is usually responsible for all budgetary, contracting, and accounting functions of an organization. In this case, the work unit should be filled with positions that primarily perform those functions such as accountants, budgeting experts, contract lawyers, etc. Once jobs are designed, the next step is to build talent development programs, performance management programs, and business processes that foster a capable workforce and organization that can meet performance expectations.

Design also must consider external forces that impact organizations, including laws, regulations, and governance requirements organizations must meet. Some functions are non-negotiable, which means work units and positions must be designed to adequately meet those requirements. This is especially true with non-profit and governmental organizations. However, all organizations are subject to some regulation, and organization design specialists benefit from being aware of the impacts these have on any client organization.

MODELS IN ORGANIZATION DESIGN

As with organization development, there are many models that a practitioner can consider when designing an organization. Most models discuss several areas like strategy, systems, talent development, performance management, and culture. There are common models like McKinsey's 7S (*Enduring Ideas: The 7-S Framework*, 2008) and Galbraith's STAR (1970), but there are also many models developed by other independent practitioners or consulting organizations. The variation in models may be attributed to a need to describe organization design relative to a specific industry (i.e., government, manufacturing, finance). What is most important is for a practitioner to be familiar with a model that applies to the organization they are working for and resonates with the key stakeholders. Design is an art, and models help guide the practitioner in the process.

As with organization development models, organization design models can apply differently to different client situations. An OD practitioner will find that many design and development models have overlapping concepts, and this goes back to the idea that design and development have a lot of intersections. Structure and job design often influence behaviors and interactions (i.e., is an organization siloed or collaborative/agile?) and similarly expected behaviors and valued behaviors can sometimes drive challenges in performance, outputs, and processes. Models help identify the root cause of potential performance issues (i.e., is it behavior, design, or both?) and by applying models appropriately, the practitioner and client can see the interlocking parts of the overall system and identify levers for change.

UNDERSTANDING ORGANIZATION DESIGN IN ORGANIZATION DEVELOPMENT

Design overlaps with organization development because of the impacts structure and processes have on behaviors within an organization. If a structure is hierarchical or siloed, it may discourage innovation, collaboration, and trust among employees and leaders. Structures are a formal recognition of how work is executed and can serve as the driver for many aspects of talent development (career progression), performance management, and recruitment practices.

Many organizations state that they are a collaborative organization that values teamwork, yet they have inadvertently established policies and systems such as a performance management program that rewards individual contribution, and the only way to get ahead is to be better than all of your peers. This system encourages competition, the lack of sharing information, and creates silos which usually leads to declining organizational performance. Their policies encourage the exact opposite of their stated objectives. Unfortunately, this is all too common. If an organization wants to encourage team performance and collaboration, then their policies, practices, and culture need to encourage that behavior, not discourage it.

Additionally, organizations that emphasize performance ratings more than talent development activities may be negatively impacting employee engagement. Modern workforce data regularly find that people seek jobs that support growth and job enrichment and that these are drivers toward overall satisfaction. Formal development programs may be designed to help encourage individual employee growth but also help the organization achieve its expected performance outcomes.

These are just a few examples of how an organization may design a structure, programs, or processes that go against the culture and behaviors it wishes to reinforce. It is important to be familiar with these programs when practicing OD because sometimes structure and/or programmatic changes may be required to make lasting culture change.

FACTORS IN ORGANIZATION DESIGN

Strategy and Systems

Organizations are created for a reason. This reason for existence is often considered the organization's purpose or mission. Everyone who has worked in an organization has probably been exposed to mission statements that are supposed to meaningfully express an organization's purpose. From that purpose, organizations move onto value statements or lists of values, which are meant to identify the behaviors and outputs the organization assigns meaning to. And finally, organizations design a vision that outlines where they expect to go from the present. All these statements and activities are intended to serve as a guiding beacon and motivator for employees as they navigate their daily work.

The problem is most organizations make these statements, hang them on the walls, distribute them in flyers, and place them on slide decks, but they do not actually live them. These statements essentially become dust collectors and fail to motivate employees to engage in their work. For the few organizations who successfully embark on providing meaning to their employees' daily work assignments, leaders are required who deeply embrace the purpose and can continuously create meaning and alignment in the work that employees do. Sometimes, this is through formal means like aligning performance standards of individuals to key performance indicators (KPIs), part of an organization's strategy, but more often it is ensuring a clear understanding of how individual work assignments help an organization achieve its mission. This understanding is most often obtained via close working relationships with leaders and subordinates who communicate frequently and effectively about work assignments.

An organization that is staffed with leaders and employees that view their work assignments as part of a job and not the execution of an overall purpose risk disengagement and reduced productivity. The disengagement from purpose could also impact an organization's culture and climate and create an atmosphere that is not effective for encouraging high performance. An OD practitioner can help an organization by identifying its mission and strategy and how its systems support them. The practitioner can also help identify if developing a mission statement is truly providing meaning and direction to the workforce, or if it is simply a "check the box" exercise that results in unread mission statements hanging on the walls.

Questions to consider:

- Does the mission align with the organization's current purpose?
- Is the mission out of date? Has the mission and purpose evolved since the establishment of the organization?
- How often does the organization evaluate its mission, vision, and values?
- How well does the organization communicate the mission, vision, and values as part of its activities?
- Does the organization's performance management, development, and other talent management systems consider its mission as part of the reason for conducting activities?
- Are employees energized by the mission and see how their contributions align with it?
- Are employees rewarded or supported for engaging in work activities that align with the mission, even if it is work that is not expected or considered part of their assignments?

Structure

The structure is the most formal representation of an organization's way of doing business. Many people align their behaviors and interactions to the structure and develop cultural norms around it. Because of this tendency, the structure plays an integral part in defining how an organization functions and executes its mission. A structure can be aligned by function, geography, purpose, or some combination of these (i.e., matrixed), but whatever the alignment, it will highly influence how an organization executes its mission. The structure is what most components of an organization will build its processes around. For these reasons, it can be critical to gain an understanding of the structure when working in organization development. An OD practitioner will learn many things about an organization's functioning simply by reviewing organization charts and recognizing how the organizations' members behave in accordance with, or perhaps despite, the organization structure.

Questions to consider:

- How does the structure support or hinder the mission?
- Are organization units based on function, geography, customer, purpose, or other methods?
- Are organization units appropriately balanced and staffed with the proper number of individuals?
- Does the organization have the right kinds of jobs to execute the purpose of organization units?
- Are organization units too top-heavy (i.e. too many leaders for the number of employees)?
- Are organization units structured in a way to encourage or discourage collaboration?
- Does the structure align to help the organization meet its objectives?

Leadership

Because of our existing organizational structures, we have created a work environment where the expected way to reward competence is to promote your best talent into management positions. While the intention for rewarding employees is likely positive, a positive outcome is not guaranteed. Organizations are increasingly reliant on knowledgeable talent to create, innovate, and design new solutions or products. The individuals capable of these activities may not have the requisite skills for leading people. If an organization's creators are best suited to the creative and innovative role, then the organization should find methods to increase rewards and responsibilities around those activities that are commensurate with other management positions.

Why is this concept so important when it comes to organization development? Simply put, promoting individuals to leadership roles who are not capable of leading people puts an organization at risk. There is nothing new in saying, "People don't leave organizations; they leave bad managers." We have all heard that statement before, so why do we keep promoting people into roles that require leading others, who are not well suited to the role? Individuals who sit in positions that require leading people and who fail to embrace this role and execute it well put many factors of organizational health at risk, including employee engagement, productivity, performance, development, and many more. Gallup's book, *It's the Manager* (Clifton & Harter, 2019), highlights many years of data collection that emphasizes that 70 percent of the organizations' effectiveness derives from its manager's performance. OD practitioners can help their organization by paying attention to how the promotion of an organization's highest performers into leadership roles is impacting the organization and by providing leadership development activities to all newly promoted leaders. Some organizations have a misguided belief that those individuals in senior leadership positions no longer need any training or development, and nothing could be further from the truth.

Questions to consider:

- Does the organization promote from within?
- Are there succession planning strategies and workforce planning strategies in place that help strategically develop staff into these roles?
- What support is provided to emerging leaders?
- What support is provided to new leaders?
- How well does an organization assess its leadership performance?
- Are leaders actively engaged in coaching, mentoring, or developing subordinate leaders?
- Does the organization structure limit or provide growth potential for knowledge and innovation leaders?
- Does the organization consider their senior experts and innovators as peers to leaders when making business decisions?

Human Capital Capabilities

An organization's ability to attract, procure, develop, and manage talent is critical to its ability to perform and execute its mission. The structure could be designed to support matrix work, developmental assignments, and other activities that allow employees to explore career interests that help execute the purpose and mission of the organization. Often there are investments in systems and processes that try to standardize work, gain efficiency, or ensure predictable financial outcomes; however, these investments are not so simple for talent since the organization does not have an easy predictive analytical outcome. As a result, many organizational leaders cannot readily speak to their benefits of investing in human capital and may avoid the investment altogether.

The OD practitioner needs to assess the extent to which an organization and its leaders are actively investing in managing its human capital capabilities and the impact of that strategy. If employees feel they are viewed as "cogs in a wheel" and are expected to produce work for little or no reward or investment in their talent, there is a likelihood that during an OD diagnostic a practitioner will find employees are not engaged in the organization's purpose, do not feel compelled to stay and grow, and will eventually be at high risk of leaving the organization. The OD practitioner may also want to review employee grievance history, turnover data, exit interview data, employee survey results, or other sources that may provide a clear understanding of the effectiveness of an organization's human capital management.

Questions to consider:

- Do recruitment practices procure the right talent for open opportunities?
- How actively are managers developing their current talent?
- Do employees have access to proper training and development activities to support their needs?
- Are employees engaged in individual development activities or are activities designed for specific jobs?
- Does the organization focus more on past performance or development?
- Are training activities aligned to developing skills required now and in the future?
- How are employees chosen for developmental activities?
- How does the organization determine the effectiveness of developmental activities? Are they assessed at all?
- Can the organization assess return on investment of development activities?

Culture

Each organization has its own unique culture comprising all the subcultures of the various locations, plants, departments, or teams. Each geographical location has its unique community or environment in which it operates, its own culturally attuned employees, and possibly its unique customers. All these variants are why there is no one model of OD or change management approach that fits all organizations, and why in large organizations it takes years, not months, to implement change.

CASE EXAMPLE

For example, consider a large health care organization which has 170 medical centers (hospitals) located all around the world, each with many departments and thousands of employees in addition to 1,063 outpatient centers also with their own employees and many departments. This is a massively interconnected system. At one point, their OD department was charged with improving the culture of the organization. Where does one even begin such a massive project?

An organization's culture is developed over time by many influencing factors. Among the more influential are the history and founding purpose of the organization, the current policies and practices, and the organization's values and leadership. The leadership and managerial style reflect the true values of the organization and influence how leadership and management use their formal authority, how they communicate with subordinates and peers alike, and all of this has a profound effect on the culture.

Executives, managers, and supervisors demonstrate the real values of the organization (as opposed to stated values) every day by how they manage or supervise. Their leadership is an unconscious demonstration of the real values of the organization. Remember what gets recognized and rewarded gets repeated.

ORGANIZATION PERFORMANCE

An organization's design should support its performance. Organizations are often driven to achieve measures, sometimes referred to as key performance indicators (KPIs). These measures serve as drivers for many business decisions and achieving (or failure to achieve) these goals may determine the individual performance decisions for senior leaders and c-suite executives. Awareness of KPIs is important because these often cascade down to the individual level. Employee performance standards then might include goals and metrics that align their job expectations to those of the organization (KPIs). This alignment helps increase transparency, clarity around expectations, and foster a sense of greater purpose for individuals.

SYSTEMS INFLUENCE

From Dictionary.com (accessed, July 17, 2021), a system is defined as "an assemblage or combination of things or parts forming a complex or unitary whole." As such, any change no matter how small affects the entire system. In many cases, the effect is negligible or minor and will not even be noticed by many other parts of the organization. For example, a change in the parking regulations will not affect those who do not drive to work and may only affect a few individuals for a short time until they get used to the new rules. In other cases, the impact is significant and greatly affects other systems within the organization (i.e., a change in the compensation system that will likely affect every employee). Sometimes these effects are anticipated and sometimes not (i.e., unintended consequences).

Organizations are living ecosystems subject to both internal and external influences. As the environment, new laws, technology, and customer preferences change, so must the company change to remain successful. As such, organizations are constantly adapting and adjusting, more recently referred to as organizational agility. These adjustments are systems changes that also affect human behavior.

Much has already been written about the effects of the various systems on human behavior, and a simple internet search will produce dozens of articles. What is common to all approaches is that the systems that an organization establishes, consciously or not, have either a positive or negative impact on the employees and customers alike. System influence may well be the strongest influence on human behavior, and it would be naive to think that the behavior employees engage in is mostly attributed to personality.

There is no single organizational system that can be applied to all organizations; however, all organizations have systems. One way to look at an organization's systems is to identify the core and supporting systems. Core systems are fundamental to the business, and if these systems are not in alignment with the mission of the organization, the organization will either be dysfunctional or go out of business. Supporting systems are the non-critical systems. While helpful in the operation of the organization, the organization could survive a certain amount of dysfunction within that system. For instance, if the communication system was not the best, the organization, while being less optimal, could survive a poor communication system. They would not likely survive a poor financial system.

Listed below are several major systems for consideration in any OD initiative. While there are others and may also be some systems specifically germane to an organization, these are a good start.

Human resource (HR) system: All organizations have an HR system whether it is formalized or not. This system is usually a major influencer of behaviors, beginning with the way the company recruits, hires, and onboards individuals. Crisis hiring often leads to crisis firing. How intentional and well thought out who is hired and when? What kind of interviewing or application process is in place and how does this affect who gets hired? Are people promoted from within or does the organization look externally for people? What kind of retention practices are in place? Why do people leave this organization and is there any theme? Who does the hiring and what effect does this have on selection? If an organization brings the wrong people in the front door in the first place, they will have ongoing people and performance problems.

- Another HR influencer is the employee handbook, company policies, practices, rules, and regulations. These all tell employees what is permissible, encouraged, and punished. It is not uncommon for organizations to have outdated policies and practices that were at one time established to overcome a problem and now are the problem.

- HR systems contain other potential influencers such as performance reviews, promotional opportunities, training, and development or career opportunities, travel, larger offices, and other forms of recognition. There is always a reason why people act the way they do, and the HR system is a powerful influencer.

The compensation system: is another strong influencer (financial compensation). Salary, bonus, and other monetary incentives guide human behavior toward maximizing performance in the areas that will help the individual obtain the most compensation. Does the organization reward individual, team, or overall organization performance with money incentives?

- Special incentives, trips, and other rewards to the higher-performing individuals or teams tend to promote competition, not collaboration, among employees.

- SEC rules, demand for growth and profitability all place demands on employees and leaders alike.

Communications system: Do people have the information they need to perform their jobs? Is the information timely and trustworthy? How transparent is the organization? Does information only come top-down, or does it flow more freely in all directions? Do communications help or hinder the organization?

Technology infrastructure: Especially at this time when more and more individuals are working from home, and this may become the new normal, does it help or hinder communications, relationship building, and productivity?

Sales and marketing systems: While not every organization has these as strong systems, they encourage a certain focus such as growth, expansion, product niche, reputation, strategic focus, etc. What, if any effect, do these systems have on human behavior?

Operational or workflow process: How is work accomplished, whether providing a service or manufacturing products? What are the steps involved in getting work done from the first customer contact to the collection of accounts receivable? How do these procedures (steps) influence what people do?

Organizational structure: A very strong influencer of human behavior is the physical properties in which people work, whether it be the area of the floor they work on or the entire campus or multiple worldwide locations. Structure limits or encourages contact, communications, relationships, and performance. With more and more people working from their personal residences, this system may not be as influential as it has been in the past; however, there is still a formal organizational chart that reflects the design of the organization and continues to influence who people report to, communicate with, etc.

SHIPYARD STORY

When conducting an organizational assessment on a major shipyard, it was discovered their overtime budget was approximately 50 percent of their total compensation paid to all employees. When asked why their overtime compensation was so high, we were told that is typical in the shipbuilding business. It was just accepted as necessary and normal. Many times, we would see people standing around waiting for something else to happen first. Sometimes it would be a scheduling issue, a safety or a union issue, a personnel issue, or any number of other issues. There was always some reason why people were standing around and unproductive. One person was taken off a ship they were working on and told to go to another ship to help. When he got to the ship, he did not know where to go or who to report to, so he stood outside of the ship until someone said, "What are you doing here?" That was two days later.

There were many blue-collar trades salaried at sixty to eighty thousand dollars per year in salary and another forty to sixty thousand dollars in overtime. They were being incentivized (financially rewarded) for not working efficiently.

ORGANIZATION CLIMATE

Assessing an organization's climate can be a major undertaking and quite complex. However, there are a few basic assessments that can be quite helpful. An obvious assessment would be to discern whether the atmosphere is predominantly positive or negative. Simply listen to the language that is used, the stories that are told, and the number of complaints or gripes people focus on. Are people focused on the past and what should or could have been done (negative), or are they focused on the future and goal setting and problem-solving (positive)?

Another assessment easily obtained through conversations, focus groups, and storytelling is the intensity of emotions that people demonstrate and whether they are acting on the emotions behaviorally or verbally. Assessing the emotional intensity will give the OD practitioner insight into the stoutness or rigidity of the climate and provide clues as to the amount of time and interventions that might be necessary to successfully implement changes in the organization as well as the level of resistance or acceptance to change that will likely be encountered.

The next assessment of the climate might identify the prevalence or strength of the climate.

POSITIVE OR NEGATIVE CLIMATE

Rarely   Sometimes   Occasionally   Considerably   Highly

In addition, it may be helpful to use two other criteria, verbal/behavioral and passive/aggressive, aggressive being stronger than passive and behavioral being more intense than verbal. Passive and neutral behaviors are more commonly found in organizations, while aggressive behaviors, either positive or negative, are not found as frequently. Aggressive verbal and/or behavioral negative clues make change considerably more difficult and frequently involve conflict resolution efforts, which must proceed any change efforts. Aggressive behaviors on the positive side demonstrate considerable caring for one another and usually take considerable effort to develop. The chart below may provide a helpful way to assess organizational climate.

NEGATIVE CLIMATE

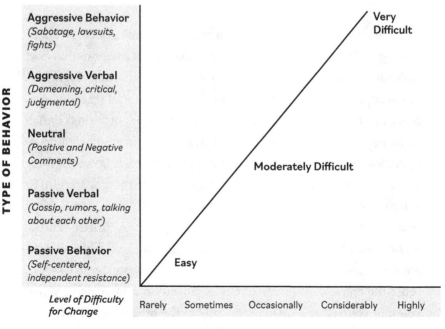

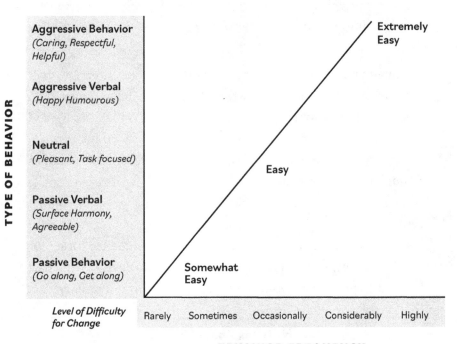

POSITIVE CLIMATE

The emotional climate of an organization influences decision-making and behaviors, so being aware of the level of emotions that exist in departmental or individual relationships is an important diagnostic. Is the organizational climate mostly positive, neutral (task-focused only), or negative? Organizations that have a history of strong conflict often must resolve the conflict and heal first before any significant operational changes can be sustainably implemented; however, there are instances where significant change, such as reorganization, or a significant crisis reduces the conflict and the need for healing first. Organizations with a positive and supportive climate tend to accommodate change with less resistance and more quickly overcome any concerns they may have. Using yourself as a barometer to gauge or sense the emotional climate of any organization is important. When you find yourself reacting emotionally to the organization, there is a good chance that others are reacting similarly. What is driving these reactions? Bringing these reactions out into the open for discussion may well be one of the more important contributions of, and role of, the OD practitioner. However, being able to do this depends considerably on how in touch with self, how emotionally aware, and how competent the practitioner is.

ORGANIZATIONAL VALUES

Many if not most organizations today have a stated set of values usually posted in conspicuous places throughout the buildings or on business cards, in annual reports, and the like. Many organizations have a set of posted values, and then there are the informal values, which are how they really behave or what is really important to them. Whenever this occurs, the informal values take precedence over the stated values (real values versus posted values).

There is a wide range of documents proclaiming to be value statements and considerable misunderstanding and confusion as to what a value is. Some value statements are simply one word, and others are run-on long paragraphs. A value is defined as worth, merit, or importance. This leaves open a wide definition for values and may contribute to the confusion. In organizational values statements, there are generally two types of values: those that define behaviors and those that define desirable traits. Those that define behavior are usually one word, and those that define traits are usually multiple words.

Honesty might be defined as candid, authentic, frank, forthright, straightforward, genuine, or other such words. Honesty is a value that will help guide behavior.

Diversity and Inclusion are more traits we wish someone to have than a value. The value may be respect or acceptance for all people.

TRAITS	BEHAVIORS
We are obsessed with communicating	Respect
	Candid / Honest
Diversity and Inclusion	
	Caring
Innovation and Creativity	
	Excellence / Quality
Support success in partnership	
	Integrity
Sports is our foundation and all that we do	Customer Service
We do the right thing	

Organizations need to be careful what they publish for mission, vision, and values statements because if they do not live up to those statements, then they usually become a source of mockery and ridicule by the employees and can become a significant negative contributor to the culture. Developing these statements usually takes time and considerable thought and is often done by senior leaders without much input from the rest of the organization. This is often why staff does not have a strong connection to these statements. Vetting them to everyone in the organization so that there is a personal connection to these statements is a critical next step.

After these statements are developed and vetted, then comes the difficult part, which is living the values and mission. This is an ongoing, never-ending process. There is a big difference in the organizational culture and employee engagement when the organization lives by their values as opposed to those that have a bunch of words on a plaque hanging on a wall in the lobby.

CONFLICT STYLE

The way conflict is handled in an organization reveals a lot about the organization's level of trust, openness, communications, the strength of relationships, emotional competence, and group maturity. In many organizations, the major way conflict is handled is avoidance. *In 1974, Kenneth W. Thomas and Ralph H. Kilmann (2007)* introduced their Thomas–Kilmann Conflict Mode Instrument (TKI). It is built along two axes, assertiveness and cooperativeness, and there are five styles of handling conflict: avoiding, accommodating, compromising, collaborating, and competing. Thomas and Kilmann are quick to point out that there is no one right style and all five have times when they might be appropriate. While this is at least a forty-five-year-old instrument, it is still a great way for a team and individuals to understand their predominant manner of dealing with conflict. Avoided conflict exacerbates distrust and closed-off communication. Hostile competing has the same effect. Since conflict is inevitable and helps groups mature past the storming stage (Truckman), the OD practitioner can be a valuable asset in helping any group, team, or organization deal with conflict productively. It is helpful if the OD practitioner is aware of their predominant style and can effectively facilitate conflict resolution sessions. Conflict resolution is not a teaching event, but a process. Roger Fisher and William Ury wrote a book called *Getting to Yes,* which is another great resource for practitioners, and it encourages understanding rather than defending a position.

Being comfortable with conflict and seeing it as a normal and healthy part of group maturation is important. The OD practitioner may choose to allow conflict to continue to see how it is resolved if it is resolved at all and who steps up to deal with the conflict. There can be unhealthy conflict, especially when it turns personal or goes beyond the stern verbal stage into the hostile or acrimonious verbal stage or the physical stages. This type of conflict must be stopped for there to be a safe environment for everyone. The practitioner's abilities and comfort with conflict are important skills.

MULTIPLE SYSTEMS

Compared to other areas of OD, little is written about working in multiple system environments. When searching the internet, what most frequently appears is multiple system atrophy (MSA), which is a neurodegenerative disease, or a computer operating system (OS) that allows multiple users on different computers to all work on the same documents at the same time. A multicultural environment tends to refer to organizations with a diverse group of people but not organizational systems. Multi-systems in OD refers to different organizational systems that influence human behavior accordingly. For example, in a multi-location organization, each organization may have different accounting practices and rules (financial system) that accounts for their financial condition. All these different systems might work well each for their own organization, but it makes it quite difficult to produce a final annual accounting or to compare locations financially.

CASE EXAMPLE

Years ago, when consulting with a mid-size organization and looking at their history, it was discovered that when a new location was established, each location had a large degree of autonomy in establishing its rules and policies. Pay rates (financial system) were established to be in line with the local community jobs of the same type, so naturally pay rates for those locations in poorer communities were lower than the same job in a location in a more well-to-do community. By way of example, the forklift operators in one location were paid significantly less than those of other locations. Unfortunately, the workforce in the poorer locations tended to be minorities while not so much in the more well-to-do locations. This meant that the organization was paying minorities less money than they were paying non-minorities doing the same job. While not intentional, this was a lawsuit waiting to happen. Once the organization realized the problems this had caused, it incorporated all pay rates into one system.

There is no doubt that organizational systems influence and may guide human behavior. Being aware of the subtleties of that influence is challenging enough, but when there are multiple different systems all within the same organization (such as different accounting methods or pay rates), it complicates the OD practitioner's work even more.

Almost all OD articles and books address the practitioner's work in a single organizational system and the larger the organization, usually the more complex the system. Today with globalization, international partnerships, mergers, acquisitions, *and* subcontractors from around the world, multiple systems are quite common. The practitioner may find themselves working with several systems all considerably different from one another and with the responsibility to help them all work well together. Different cultures, labor laws, mores, leadership styles, and organizational size and structures challenge any practitioner's integration abilities. In small and mid-size companies, when buying a competitor as a strategy for market growth, it is quite common to leave the purchased company with its old name, leadership, and culture. In these cases, the parent company may own dozens of very different companies all operating quite independently of one another. There is no single system. Even transferring from one company to the next is a bit of a cultural shock that takes some getting used to. At what point, if ever, does the company decide to operate as one company with one culture and leadership style or continue as a patchwork of organizations with only a fiscal responsibility to headquarters?

Multiple systems create additional complexities for everyone, and the OD practitioner's skill in adjusting the design and delivery of programs to fit the existing circumstances creates at a minimum additional work and challenges for the practitioner. The OD practitioner will likely want to consider the appropriateness of different cultures and climates throughout a multiple system organization. For example, a company that has a headquarters in the US and a headquarters in Asia will to some extent demonstrate different cultural behaviors and norms, as would be expected. However, what is important is to identify how those two headquarters are expected to behave across cultures to constructively manage the organization in consideration of those two systems. This balancing and integration of the two cultures is no easy task and yet would be important when determining the strategic direction of a company that has multiple systems.

EXAMPLE

What would you do if a rather large provider of consumer goods with international sales embarked on a quality improvement program because they were receiving many costly returns, which affected their profitability by about 4 to 6 percent? Improved profitability and improved quality leading to improved customer satisfaction were the identified goals of this initiative. They asked the internal OD (single person) practitioner who was assigned to the Training and Development division of the HR department (and they reported to the operations director) to oversee this initiative and to make recommendations on how to proceed. While they had several manufacturing groups that produced their own products, many other groups were not manufacturing anything but providing final assembly of parts made elsewhere. They also had several products that were partially made in one facility and then completed in another, encouraging long transportation time and distances in some cases. They also had products that were major sellers in some countries that were made in other countries, even though the first country had manufacturing capabilities, but they were often busy making parts for products sold in other countries.

The corporate structure was such that there were companies directly owned by Headquarters, some that were in partnership, some franchise entities, some very independent with only a supply commitment to the main company. Some companies were in countries that had high quality standards and others in countries with no quality standards. Some were in countries with strict export requirements and others with very loose requirements. Each company seemed to have a different culture and leadership style. They wanted to purchase one of their better suppliers in Taiwan; however, they were told by the State Department to be careful due to China's claimed ownership. This warning put this entire process on hold and threatened the supply line.

Communications were often difficult due to time differences around the world, lack of integrated technology, and different languages. Supply line and logistics challenges were a daily occurrence with very high costs for stockpiling parts for emergencies. Performance, quality, customer service, profitability, and other major indicators all varied greatly between the business entities. There was no accountability nor consequence for poor performance. Parts they received were often late or of poor quality, and many suppliers were highly inconsistent. Turnover in their own manufacturing facilities was low except in a few where it was quite high due to the leadership of these departments. EEO and employee complaints were also high in these same facilities.

Closing a few locations was earlier deemed a good move, but finance said the tax consequences along with the moving costs and retraining costs cancelled any short-term benefit, so consolidation was also placed on hold.

Conducting an assessment to determine that there were tremendous differences in cultures, operations, and systems was deemed to be a waste of time since this was already known.

Where do you begin?

While having multiple systems increases the complexity of any change initiative or program implementation, the following first few steps may be helpful.

- Establish a common goal across the entire organization. The goal is often tied to the mission or purpose of the organization.
- Establish a core set of values that would cross most, if not all, cultures.

- Develop appropriate cross-cultural steering committees or project teams to work on mutually beneficial issues.
- Celebrate the cultural differences as a strength, not an impediment.
- Focus on the customer, for without them, the organization would not need to exist.
- Provide cross-training opportunities that aid in both individual skill development and increase exposure to different cultures and operations.
- If necessary, break up large projects into different locations and deal with individual cultures and issues in the short term.
- Focus on improvements, not locations or cultural differences, yet be aware of how those differences affect the problem.

FUTURE OF ORGANIZATION STRUCTURES

Not so long ago, the environment was filled with technology integration and cloud computing, which was going to change the way we worked and how we were organized. Then the push came from artificial intelligence (AI), which was going to require significant retraining and reskilling. Now the pandemic is going to change organizations as more and more people work from home. The environment is constantly changing and at an ever-increasingly rapid rate, which is forcing organizations to be in a constant state of adaptation. The oxymoron "constant change" has never been truer.

What does this all mean for future organization designs, for the current top-down hierarchical model? Ever since Fredrick Taylor's theories emerged in 1911, we have been attempting to make the top-down model more effective. For the last 220 years, this has been the main model of organization for the entire world, and it will not likely go away easily since it is ingrained in all facets of our lives. There may be appropriate places for this model such as in the military or paramilitary professions, or during a crisis or war, but it is evident that is not a good model for creativity, employee engagement, and issues like creating a passionate workforce. The top-down model creates a central control group with the remainder of the workforce merely following orders. Being a high-performing, efficient organization today will be hampered by the top-down model. A different way of working will require a different way of organizing the digital world. The rapid adaptations required of digital work are not supported by the usually rigid top-down model. The rigid approval processes usually seen in the top-down model will no longer work due to their usually slow nature.

Developing and adopting a new organization design is difficult, takes time for employees to accept, and may be subject to trial and error. According to *The Organization of the Future Arriving Now* (Deloitte.com, accessed July 17, 2021), "many organizational redesigns fail because they are reduced to an exercise to cut costs. Further they report that up to 70 percent of reorganizations fall short because of 'creative disobedience' from the executive team." Letting go of the power and control of the top-down model will not be easy for the executives at the top, it will be a challenge to all that they know and do. We spend significantly more time with people near our desk than with people far away from us, and now we might spend more electronic time with people than in-person time. Whatever the case, work tends to get done best in smaller groups. In today's world, these smaller groups will have to develop and disband rapidly as the work dictates. Instead of a top-down model, we may need more of a team-centric model. In a survey by Deloitte, 94 percent of the companies report that "agility and collaboration" are critical to their organization's success, yet only 6 percent say that they are "highly agile today"; 19 percent describe themselves as "not agile."

Further, it will likely be easier for smaller organizations to adapt than larger ones, for more recently formed organizations than organizations with a long history, and for certain types of industries over others. There likely will be many trials and errors and many failed experiments (unintended consequences), and there may be multiple models that work rather than a one-size-fits-all approach.

A new organization structure will likely require a different type of leadership and the best leader of the organization currently may not be what is needed for the new organization structure. Just as employees need to be more agile, so will the leadership. If the team is truly self-directed with all working toward a common goal, will there be any need for leadership at all? Building teams and providing oversight may be the leader's new job rather than the traditional way of making decisions and giving out work assignments.

In the future, it may be not *who do you work for*, but *who do you work with*; not *what do you do*, but *what is your current project*; not *who is your boss*, but *how do decisions get made*. Regardless of what structure an organization adopts, there will be system effects on the employees, and there will be a need for human habits and behaviors to change.

CONCLUSION

This chapter discusses topics that relate to both organization design and organization development that a practitioner may want to consider. Organization design models, like organization development models, exist to help the practitioner discuss the whole system through an appropriate framework. A practitioner will want to be able to differentiate when a cause of challenges is attributed to a design issue, a behavior issue, or some combination of both. Sometimes, a change to the design will positively and greatly influence the behaviors in an organization. By understanding how structure, systems, and processes influence behavior, an OD practitioner will increase their ability to assess the whole system influencing an organization.

DISCUSSION QUESTIONS

- How does structure influence behavior in organizations (or in your own organization)?
- What elements of design would you want to consider assessing when conducting a diagnostic?
- How would you factor in multiple systems concerns when working with a client?
- What would have to happen in your organization for alternative organizational structures (i.e., less bureaucratic) to work?
- How do your leaders impact the organization's culture?
- How are your senior leaders contributing to the problems?
- How are your senior leaders contributing to the solution?
- Is your culture more positive or negative and how did it get that way?
- What are your organization's values and how are they lived?
- What one structure or design change would have a profound impact on performance?

CHAPTER FIVE

Organizational Change

INTRODUCTION

The focus of this chapter is on change within an organization. Change topics are broken into three main discussion topics: client readiness, factors influencing change, and the practitioner's role in managing change. In this chapter, we focus more on the difficulties often associated with organizational change. We look at why so many OD initiatives fail, including quick fixes, the client's readiness for change, senior-level support, the 51 percent concept and ownership, factors that affect successful organizational change, the level of resistance to change, red flags, determining root cause, and measuring the cost of the problem.

Change management is a discipline applied to managing change initiatives and is often overlapped with the concept of OD. However, these two concepts are not one and the same. The OD practitioner plays a vital role in identifying when a client is truly ready for change, how to identify the factors that will positively or negatively influence change efforts, and applying sound OD techniques to influence change. Change management helps structure the change initiative, but the root of success with change is in identifying those behaviors that need to change and designing interventions to support that change, activities that typically belong with an OD practitioner.

FAILED INITIATIVES

Fifty to seventy percent of all organizational change initiatives do not meet all their stated goals (John Kotter, 1995, and McKinsey, 2010). This does not bode well for any practitioner's reputation and further discourages both organizations and employees alike. Sustainable organizational change is a complex, interconnected process that takes years, not months, and there are many obstacles and pitfalls to resolve, sometimes daily. Added to that, the unintended and unforeseen consequences of change itself and the constantly changing environment to which the organization must respond requires the practitioner to constantly deal with symptoms and consequences of change. The practitioner will always be looking for root cause and system influences to resolve issues and support healthy change. Additionally, the practitioner will be building trusting relationships throughout the organization, while simultaneously navigating difficult personalities. This is a bit of a challenge, but that is also the excitement of being an OD practitioner and helping an entire organization and all of its employees improve. Why such a high failure rate? Here are a few of the more common reasons:

- Isolated implementation rather than an integrated systems approach.
- Lack of senior leadership support.
- Lack of senior leadership willingness to change themselves.
- Inadequate resource allocation.
- Lack of employee involvement at all levels.
- High levels of resistance to change.
- High levels of unresolved conflict.
- Inadequate and inconsistent communication.

- Insufficient time (organizational change almost always takes longer and costs more than anticipated).
- Distraction from primary focus with "other duties as assigned," especially for internal OD practitioners; also scope creep (project expansion), especially for external OD practitioners.
- Organizational structure, culture, leadership style, or policies and practices do not support or work against the change initiative.

Also, some projects are doomed to fail from the beginning, and the OD practitioner needs to be aware of the expectations of management and the deliverables they would be responsible to produce. Often the lack of allocated resources stems from a lack of understanding of the enormousness of what it takes to produce sustainable organizational change. A good rule of thumb to remember is that organizations do not and cannot change. Organizations are a concept, people change, and when people change, so does the organization. Organizational change is changing the systems, policies, and practices that influence human behavior and behavioral change. Both take time and considerable reinforcement.

Often senior leadership is among the key people that need to change. Assume that senior leadership is always part of the problem. This is not to blame them, but it is to say that this is a normal condition. Their part in the problem is that they may have allowed, tolerated, endured, or put up with the problem for years and thus have become the enablers. At the same time, senior leadership is always part of the solution as well. Their involvement is necessary for the change initiative to succeed. Sometimes the most significant contribution senior leadership can make is to change themselves, change how they behave, how they lead, how they tolerate, or how they endure problems. Sometimes it is senior leadership that needs to be changed before there are any reasonable expectations that the organization itself will change. These are the difficult situations the OD practitioner may find themselves embroiled in.

Another important reason for the high failure rate is the solution is already decided and given to the OD practitioner to help implement before any due diligence is conducted and determining appropriate employee involvement. Often, the given solution is an event while organizational change is always a process. Further, the given solution tends to address a performance or behavioral problem (singular cause) and may not be addressing the causal factors.

Many times, organizations do not see the need for further diagnosis and want a quick fix. OD practitioners, to be effective, must be temperate in their implementation of quick fixes, as well as realistic in their limited benefits. Quick fixes are often exactly what the organization is requesting and usually not what the organization needs to sustainably improve. Quick fixes may or may not fix an immediate problem but rarely address the system influences that contributed to the problem in the first place.

Remember that people behave in ways the system encourages them to behave. While well-intended, quick fixes often are not sustainably effective. While there may be short-term or individual benefits, there is little organization improvement or system-wide sustainable change that occurs. Sometimes their solutions were tried before and did not work, so what will be different this time? Other times, the solution might address the individual behaviors without changing the process or system, so individuals will likely revert to what the system encourages. At other times, their solution might address the rules and policies without supporting behavioral change. Many times, their solution is a training program for a certain group even when the lack of skills is not a problem. Being alert to these simple solutions and recommending a deeper analysis is one of the critical skills the OD practitioner brings to the organization and is invaluable.

CASE EXAMPLE

Organization "A" experienced increased customer complaints, cost overruns, failure to meet delivery dates to customers, increased rework on the shop floor, and quality issues. Management discussed the issues and determined that critical information was not passed on from department to department in a timely fashion or at all. Without shared information, the various departments were not cooperating nor collaborating well, and each department seemed to have a different set of priorities. Work was chaotic at best, which in part contributed to quality issues, long work cycles, and high personnel turnover.

The lack of communications took center stage, and it was determined by senior management that all managers would attend a communications training program to improve the communications between their respective departments. Various programs were reviewed, and a vendor was chosen to deliver the content. Included in the program was training in areas such as listening, sending "I" messages, morning meetings, passing on information, transparency, and written notices. Some of the skills were individual skills, and others were more suited for organizational or team implementation. It was a two-day program implemented by an outside vendor but managed and organized by the OD-HR. Follow up was to be the OD practitioner's responsibility.

The training was considered successful and 86 percent of all managers attended (some on leave or sick when training was offered) and evaluations were generally good, however, very little change occurred. For about *two* weeks after the conclusion of the training program, there were increased attempts and increased communications, and then everything went back to "normal." The system influences were stronger than individual efforts. The natural consequences of any failed training program are blaming the training, the trainer, and/or the follow-up; employees more frustrated and believing that nothing will ever change around here; employees more resistant to the next training program or change initiative;

wasted time, money, and opportunity costs.

Had the organization asked the OD practitioner to assess why the communications are poor, they may have discovered far more critical issues that needed to be addressed.

A. The organization had a strong top-down model of management, which encouraged strong silos. There was little collaboration between the silos.

B. Knowledge in this organization was power, so there was little sharing of information in the silo and even less between silos.

C. There was a strong culture of competition between the silos and large financial rewards for the best performing division. The financial system supported non-cooperation.

D. There were managerial relationships that were highly conflictual due to a long history of untrustworthy behaviors.

E. The focus was on getting the job done at all costs, and improving relationships was considered soft and nonessential. Most managers were task-focused, not relationship focused.

F. While the organization verbalized their customer service concerns, most attention was paid to financial numbers and getting product out the door.

G. Quality was also stated as one of the organization's values, but because of their focus on the numbers, the motto in the shipping room was "if it fits in the box, ship it."

H. The physical structure of the plant and organization of the divisions put some groups that needed close cooperation the furthest away from one another, discouraging communications and contact.

All this feedback was readily available and came from the employees, who were never brought into the discussion. Had management done so, they might not have spent a considerable amount of time and money on an unneeded training program.

There is a large and constantly growing body of knowledge available for OD practitioners. If you are emerging from a graduate program to a practitioner role, you will have obtained quite a bit of foundational knowledge of theories and organization systems; and if you're new to the field with no formal education, you'll find plenty of books, articles, and journals espousing discussion about organization development. All this knowledge, while important, is put to the test upon entering a practitioner role. The OD practitioner is responsible for observing human behaviors in the context of the organizational system to determine the best approach to make meaningful and lasting organizational change.

If organizational and human behavior change were easy, there would be no need for OD practitioners. Practitioners must constantly navigate a changing environment. The OD practitioner is faced with numerous and often different departmental requirements and unrealistic deadlines. The OD practitioner is always on the lookout for unintended consequences before and after implementation. They must deal with difficult personalities and nonbelievers as well as overly optimistic and enthusiastic individuals, with authoritarian leaders, declining budgets, limited resources, complex interconnected problems with significant organizational consequences, and with constantly changing customer demands. Additionally, they also must be aware of organizational politics and avoid the pressure of everyone wanting someone else to change. Also, OD consultants are often dealing with people who . . .

- do not necessarily get along with each other;
- do not tell you the facts but tell you their version of the facts;
- are afraid to tell you truthfully how they feel and think and withhold information from you;
- have significant conflict, sometimes many years old;
- are senior management and are part of the problem;

- do not want anything to change as bad as it is;
- believe that the decisions and wisdom come from the top down and fail to involve those at the working level;
- may want a mechanical approach rather than a people-centric approach;
- want to implement a lot of new rules and regulations, which might end up signifying their low trust level of the workforce;
- focus mainly on the economics of the organization rather than improving the workforce, or the structure and design rather than the culture.

When the senior team is myopic about what they want to see in their change initiative, or they do not see the connections to other elements of the system, it often becomes difficult for the OD practitioner to encourage a broader scope and spend more time and money. Countless efforts fail because the senior team does not involve the people who will be most affected by the change.

Add to this list of challenges your own lack of personal experience and knowledge in certain areas and your reliance on those that have the requisite skills/knowledge. While this list is not necessarily comprehensive, it makes the case that the practitioner must be sensitive to the people. A practitioner who is sensitive can learn to navigate a constantly changing environment, with constantly evolving relationships and requirements.

These are but a few of the many reasons why OD initiatives fail to achieve sustainable organizational improvements. We now turn our attention to client readiness for change.

CLIENT READINESS

Even when a client initiates the request for a change initiative, that does not mean that they are ready to change. Sometimes the most well-intentioned client will affirm they are ready for change but, once the work begins, will shy away from the process and ultimately lose momentum. Momentum can be lost for a variety of reasons, but emerging (new) business priorities often derails clients from engaging in long-term OD change initiatives.

Then there is the question of ready for what?

Many times, the OD practitioner is contacted by a client and given a solution to implement. In these instances, a client is being prescriptive based on their understanding of the situation which may or may not include a causal or system analysis. A good diagnostic process would identify either the root causes or multiple causes of the problem. If a client calls with a solution, often someone in authority decides that a specific type of training program or intervention will fix or improve a condition or problem within the organization without doing a root cause assessment. Nevertheless, the OD practitioner is given a task to implement a given program/initiative. At this point, the OD practitioner will need to decide if the given solution is really the solution to the organization's issue or if it is merely a Band-Aid or a temporary fix, or maybe not a fix at all. Once someone has decided on a given course of action, it is often difficult to change their minds with reason alone; they may be emotionally attached to the given solution or in worst-case scenarios have a friend or vested personal interest in having an outside firm provide the solution. Instead of focusing on the given solution, it may help the OD practitioner to focus on the goal or desired outcome the organization is seeking, then be able to identify what is supporting the current situation and what it will take to go from the current situation to the desired outcome. There is great risk in a prescriptive approach with change initiatives. Research shows that up to 70 percent of OD initiatives fail (Beer & Nohria, 2000), and according to a summary article from BD Academy (accessed July 25, 2021), measures of training effectiveness show the following:

- Even when training is liked by participants, only 37 percent of it led to learned new skills, just 13 percent was relevant to the workplace, and only 3 percent had an impact on the company (Association of Training & Development).
- Up to 80 percent of new skills are lost within one week of formal training if not used (ATD).
- 87 percent of new skills acquired are lost within a month of training (Xerox).
- 90 percent of new skills learned from corporate training are lost within a year (*Wall Street Journal*).
- Continuous training (at least ten months) results in a 50 percent increase in sales return per participant (Brevet).
- $13.5m is lost per year per one thousand employees due to ineffective training (Grovo).
- Only 20 percent of training shows transfer of learning or impact a company's bottom line (Tannenbaum).
- Up to 85 percent of sales training fails to deliver a positive ROI (HR Chally).
- Only 38 percent of managers believe training programs meet their learner's needs (ATD).

Why do up to 70 percent of OD initiatives fail to meet their stated goals and only 3 percent of the organizations receive benefits from training programs? These numbers are not random. There are reasons for this dismal performance.

Why would any organization want to implement a change initiative with such poor success rates? These success rates make the case for encouraging a client to spend a little time and money defining the root cause and planning for a successful implementation first rather than spending a lot of time and money implementing something that does not need to be implemented or that addresses the wrong problem. The lesson here is to remember the process of OD and ensure change initiatives are addressing the root causes of problems and not the symptoms. So how does the OD practitioner determine if the client is ready for change? Here are a few helpful questions:

- How are they defining the change? What specifically are they requesting?
- Are there sufficient resources and time allocated to this project?
- Are they willing to work on other related issues if they arise?
- What is their motivation for change? What is driving this request?
- Where does this initiative fit in with all of their other activities?
- How high up did this request originate from?
- What obstacles do they foresee that may get in the way?

SETTING THE STAGE FOR CHANGE

Ensure Senior Level Support

Senior-level support is essential for all organizational change initiatives as these initiatives take valuable resources (i.e., time, people, money) away from other efforts deemed important by the organization. Without senior-level support, the likelihood that the project will be successful or sustained is minimal. Change from the bottom-up rarely works for the long term and at the very least is considerably more difficult and takes more time. To ensure senior-level support, it is important to first identify all the employees and teams that will be affected by the change program. Then the practitioner can identify all senior leaders responsible for those employees and teams and engage in conversations that encourage them to actively support the initiative. In some instances, the practitioner will need to spend significant time working with senior leaders to change their culture and climate first before engaging in initiatives that more broadly engage employees. This investment in senior leaders will pay dividends in supporting successful change because employees will not usually behave in ways that senior leaders do not. If senior leaders can model the changes they seek before engaging in broad change initiatives, then employees may see more value in trusting the change initiative.

In addition to seeking senior leaders to model the behavior changes, they should also be responsible for creating a sense of urgency around the project to help motivate staff and be visually present as often as necessary during the change process. Senior leaders will have to constantly and transparently express support for the changes, have a dominant elevator speech, at least for the short term until change efforts gain momentum. To encourage and accomplish successful change, senior leaders are "a" and may be "the" critical element in the process; thus, it is always beneficial to gain the highest level of support possible.

51 Percent Concept

Something is terribly wrong if the OD practitioner has more investment and motivation for the change than the client. If this is the case, change will likely not be successful because as soon as the practitioner leaves, so does the motivation for change. As a rule of thumb, the client must have at least 51 percent of the responsibility (ideally a lot more) for change, and the long-term ownership must rest with the client. As soon as the OD practitioner senses that they want the change more than the client, it is time to stop the initiative and put the issue of ownership on the table for candid discussion. At this moment, it may be time to stop the initiative altogether, that priorities have changed, or that the client never really wanted change in the first place but felt compelled to do so for several reasons that were not truly compelling. If not stopping the initiative, it may be time to alter the initiative or time to recommit to the initiative. As a practitioner, remember that it is best not to go where you are not wanted. Work with those clients that want to improve, not with those whose goal is to resist or defeat the changes. There may be times when walking away from an initiative might be the best thing the practitioner can do for an organization. To encourage an organization not to waste their time and money on a project that will either not be successful in the long term or only give the organization minimal results not commensurate with the effort and expenditure of resources is a valuable contribution the OD practitioner can make.

Momentum can shift throughout any change process; thus, the 51 percent rule of thumb is not hard and fast. Often the investment from the client may fluctuate throughout the life of the process; the client may place an increased dependency on the practitioner early in the process and then become more independent later. However, when the client's motivation and momentum begin to wane, the OD practitioner can be enormously helpful in bringing this to light and then work with the client to mutually determine what next steps are warranted and appropriate. There are many reasons why momentum is difficult to sustain, and the loss of drive or energy on longer-term initiatives is quite normal and should be expected. Momentum loss usually results in more dependence on the practitioner. To counter this, the practitioner can help the client gain short-term successes or develop an internal support system for the initiative that can be called upon when necessary.

In addition to momentum shifts, it is also quite common for leadership to transfer ownership of the issue, either unconsciously or consciously, to the OD practitioner. Simple statements such as "we want you to . . ." or "can you help us accomplish . . ." are subtle ways to transfer ownership to the practitioner. Early in the contracting phase, or occasionally in the initial contact, ownership of the current situation needs to be discussed. OD practitioners are conductors that orchestrate a process, they are not miracle workers. Transferring and keeping the balance of ownership with the appropriate individuals/ groups is not a one-time discussion. Instead, it is an ongoing process that requires frequent calibration throughout the life of a project. Regardless of whether you are an internal or external practitioner, it is never your organization: the practitioner is there to help both individuals and organizations be better.

Transferring or developing ownership within the employee ranks is more difficult than imagined or anticipated. There is learned helplessness with the top-down model and natural deference to authority. There is also the "that's not my job" mantra echoed by many who do not want to take responsibility. Some employees are strongly ingrained to follow orders that when given the chance to be self-directing are unable to do so. They do not have the skills, knowledge, or inclination.

CLIENT EXERCISE: ENCOURAGING OWNERSHIP

A simple exercise to encourage an organization to own its culture starts with having a group of executives and/or employees identify the current organizational culture in three words or less. Participants in this exercise anonymously and individually write their three words on an index card or piece of paper. The practitioner then collects the papers and asks two participants from the client organization to write the words on two separate lists (preferably on a whiteboard where all can see). One list includes positive words and the other negative. If it is unclear whether a word is meant to be positive or negative, it is placed on both lists. Generally, there is a mix of both positive and negative words, but sometimes the list is more heavily weighted toward one side or the other. Once the list is complete, the practitioner asks the group if this is a realistic assessment of the current culture. This is an easy and quick organizational assessment.

Regardless of what the words say, the practitioner can add some levity to the exercise and tell the group, "There is good news: at 5 p.m., *I get to go home.*" Usually, participants laugh, and while some humor is appreciated, the intent in saying this is to remind the group that this is the home they created. The practitioner can remind the group that they cannot go home because this is what they come to every day: *t*his is their culture. Right at this point, we are transferring the responsibility for the organization, problem, or process to the group. If they like all the listed words, they probably do not have to change anything, but if they do not like some of the words, we now have a baseline.

The next step would be to have the group create a vision of what they would like to see in six to *twelve* months and what would be realistic to achieve. We then have an assessment of the current situation and a vision for a future organization. Now, all we need to do is identify the steps to get from A to B.

This simple yet powerful exercise transfers responsibility to the client and gets the process moving.

ORGANIZATIONAL CHANGE

Organizational change is not a repetitive process (cookie cutter). Each OD intervention is different. Cultural and organizational change is a messy and constantly evolving process, and mistakes will be made. That is the norm. Obstacles and unforeseen problems always occur. No matter how much you plan, there are always surprises.

Organizational and cultural change initiatives often take years, not months. Many factors will lengthen the amount of time necessary for successful and sustainable change.

- Size

  - If an organization is under two hundred employees, significant change can be accomplished in six to eighteen months. Small organizations are generally more flexible and the interconnectedness of their systems far less complex than larger organizations. A caveat here is if an organization has a long history of a negative culture, it may take longer to move from the inertia and negativity developed over time.

- ○ If an organization is between 200 and 2,000 employees, a two to four-year timeframe is more realistic.

- ○ If an organization has 2,000 to 10,000 employees, at least three to six years will be necessary.

- ○ If an organization has 10,000 or more employees, it is not uncommon to be looking at a ten-year or longer timeframe for organizational change.

- Geography

  - ○ Organizations that are spread all over the world with many different cultural norms are far more difficult than an organization of similar size in a single location and with a common culture.

- Diversity of Business

  - ○ The number of diverse businesses within the organization is also a factor. The more diversity of business, the more complex the change initiative, and the longer the timeframe necessary.

- Conflict History

  - ○ Organizations with a history of internal or external conflict generally must resolve the conflict (heal and forgive) before they can accommodate new changes. Conflict can, and often does, add to the time necessary for change.

- Leadership Style

    o A toxic leadership style is a large impediment to change, and it is not uncommon to spend one to three years working with just senior leaders when toxic leadership is present. Once there is a more benign or participatory leadership style in place, then the work of organizational change can take place.

- Compliance/Rebellion

    o The more dictatorial or autocratic the leadership style, the more hierarchical the organization, the more rebellious or compliant the employees. Rebelliousness tends to foster significant interpersonal conflict, competition, and hostilities, while compliance tends to foster learned helplessness, obedience, withdrawal, and a lack of creativity. Both can be destructive to organizational health. Assessing the compliance/ rebellion level is an important diagnostic and will aid the OD practitioner in the development and delivery phases.

- Other Priorities

    o Keeping a focus on the original initiative is difficult in fast-paced and constantly changing environments. When there are many different priorities, resources can easily be shifted to the most critical priority of the moment and then shifted back at a later date or never shifted back at all.

- Leadership Changes

    o When senior leaders sponsor an initiative, leave an organization, or receive different responsibilities, projects are often threatened. Unless new senior leadership takes over the sponsorship with the same degree of commitment or higher as previous leadership, momentum will likely be lost and the change effort ended.

- Unrealistic Timeframes

    o Many organizations establish timetables that are aggressive or unrealistic. As a result, the OD practitioner has increased pressure to hurry or rush the project at the initial cost of quality and the long-term costs of effectiveness and sustainability.

- Financial Constraints

    o An organization may have only funded a diagnostic phase or funded enough for a beginning change initiative; thus, the OD practitioner will have to exit the change initiative before any substantial and sustaining changes occur.

- Communication/Motivation

    o The client is responsible for communicating the changes and the results to everyone and keeping everyone motivated and involved. This is usually not the OD practitioner's responsibility. Ideally there will be an internal project manager or a lead person who will take on these responsibilities even if the OD practitioner is internal. This is a part of building an infrastructure that will support the changes and ensure sustainability. Frequent communication during times of change is extremely important, and the communications are best when they come from multiple levels, including senior management. Reporting the successful efforts is highly motivating to all.

- Other Factors

  o Many other factors will lengthen the time necessary for the successful implementation of a change initiative. Any major disruption to the planned schedule will likely cause time delays. The ability of a practitioner to be flexible and adapt to the circumstances that influence a change initiative is critical to supporting clients.

RESISTANCE TO CHANGE

You have to change minds before you can change behaviors. Once a paradigm is formed, we do not have to spend a lot of conscious energy to think things through, and then our behaviors follow our thinking. So, to change behaviors, we may have to change how people think first.

Resistance to change can be relentless because it may well be a protective mechanism deeply ingrained in our brain structures. Change requires us to think in new ways, and because change requires more conscious energy, there is a natural resistance to it. When it comes to our brains, social pain and physical pain are the same, and because change tends to bring up fear or safety issues, your brain will naturally default to protect itself and resist the change. Additionally, change tends to create stress, which exacerbates the change process and increases resistance to change.

The OD practitioner may assume that there will always be resistance to any change; the question is how much resistance. The OD practitioner will need to assess the resistance level and its causation. Where is this resistance coming from and why?

Here are some basic concepts around levels of resistance:

- Very light resistance

    o   The problems are far more painful than the anticipated change, so any resistance is generally not due to the issues; instead, resistance is due to learning something new, which takes time and energy. Also, in this case, the majority of people will be on board with the changes, while there may be a few individuals that resist more strongly. There are more optimists than skeptics.

- Light resistance

    o   There may be a fair amount of concern, often due to lack of information. While some individuals may be more vocal than others, once the need for change is explained, many will begin to support the process. There will be skeptics, but most quickly become either neutral or supporters once involved. This level of resistance is to be expected.

- Resistance

    o   This level of resistance may be referred to as normal resistance. In addition to the skeptics, there are cynics. Some of the skeptics will remain skeptical throughout the change process, and some will become supporters. The cynics, however, tend to be destructive to the process and either consciously or unconsciously work to stop the change. At this phase, it is normal to hear some individuals bad-mouthing the change initiative or program; however, the resistance is more passive than active. This negativity can slow or stymie the change initiative and will need to be addressed.

- Heavy resistance

  o At this stage, there are more cynics than skeptics, and
     the resistance is more pervasive than localized. The
     resistance is more active than passive, and in addition
     to verbal resistance, there is also observable behavioral
     resistance. This level of resistance cannot be ignored.

- Very heavy resistance

  o At this level, there is a lot of behavioral resistance,
     even to the point of sabotage. There is extremely heavy
     verbal and behavioral resistance, and the success of
     any change process is minimal at best. Usually, at this
     level, there is a long history of resistance to change as
     well. There is a far greater chance of failure than there
     is of success. The practitioner would be wise to either
     not proceed with the change or readjust their plans to
     only deal with the resistance at this time.

When dealing with resistance to change, it is important to
differentiate between those who are champions of the change
initiative, those who are skeptical of it, and those who are categorically
resistant. The support that can be gleaned from believers, and those
skeptics who engage in the process, will be valuable to continuing
the effort. If the client is demonstrating mostly heavy resistance,
it may be appropriate to pause the effort and encourage the client
to consider how invested it is in the change. One other option to
consider is if the organization needs to truly change people (i.e.,
change leaders) in order to enact any meaningful change. There are
many options for navigating resistance to change, but having allies
in the client organization is critical to success.

RED LIGHTS

When working with a client, a practitioner will need to remain alert to red lights that show challenges to the change process. The practitioner can help a client navigate past resistance by addressing red flags as they arise.

Stoplights have three different color lights that mean different things. Green for go, yellow for slow down, and red for stop. Using that color coding that same concept can be applied to conversations. Many times, we might hear or see something that throws up a yellow or red light. Do you tend to slow down or stop the conversation or ignore it and continue? Bringing up the subtle and at times unintended communications that may indicate current or future problems is one way the OD practitioner can provide a valuable service to the client. As a practitioner, if you see, hear, smell, or sense it, say it: bring the red or yellow light up for discussion. For example, upon hearing several very valid and logical reasons why not to proceed, the consultant can say, "I hear your reasons for not proceeding, and they are very logical reasons, but I am also sensing a reluctance to move forward on this as well. Am I reading this right or am I off base here?" or "If we could address your concerns to your satisfaction would you still want to proceed or not?"

Many times, individuals may not be conscious of the message they are communicating, and when brought up to consciousness, it gives them a chance to clarify their intentions. At other times, it brings up issues that they were hoping to hide and now must deal with. This is all a part of being honest, candid, and transparent with one another and is a critical component of building trusting relationships and navigating change. This requires the OD practitioner to be sensitive to the environment, observant of little nuances that occurred in communications, and be able to articulate that which is not spoken. This is both a skill and an art form. The art form comes in when bringing up that which is not spoken in a nonthreatening manner. By doing so, the practitioner will assist the client in overcoming resistance to change.

Another issue is problem clarity or definition. The same word may have different meanings for everyone involved. What does "improve" mean? Does it mean we are doing more of something or less of something? What specifically is the goal or desired outcome? What is it the organization wants to improve/fix? Be specific. Specificity leads to goal attainment, while generality leads to goal failure.

- What do we want to see more or less of?
- What specific behaviors need to change?
- What is the ultimate end goal?
- What is supporting the current situation?
- Who needs to be involved?

ROOT CAUSE

The term denotes the earliest, most basic, "deepest" cause for a given behavior, the beginning or origins of a problem or condition. There is always a reason why something is the way it is. Very few organizational conditions are random. Instead, many organizational conditions are institutionalized and have become part of the brick and mortar, so they seem quite normal and a part of the history of the organization, a "that's the way it's always been done" mentality. Along with that mentality often comes learned helplessness.

History has shown different implications for external and internal practitioners. The benefit of being an external practitioner is that they are not as acculturated to those conditions and can often see them for what they are. Whereas internal OD practitioners have to be constantly questioning and asking "why" these conditions exist and does it help or hinder the organization accomplish its mission. Unless the root cause of problems is addressed, it is likely that any changes that are made or training provided will not be sustainable in the long run and could further the negative consequences of the existing problem and further reinforce negativity toward change.

A good organizational assessment and analysis of the data will uncover many opportunities for improvement, some more serious and urgent than others. Often, the areas that need the most improvement were not a part of the original charter or request. For instance, the diagnostic may have been designed to uncover the reason for the high turnover in one department only to find out that the turnover is due to autocratic and demanding managers and to further discover that the managers are the way they are because of both production demands placed on them and past policies and rules. However, the high turnover could have been caused at least in part by any number of other factors:

- Bad hiring practices
- Increased sales, therefore, increased production demands
- A culture of a high focus on task accomplishments low focus on people
- Poor onboarding
- Reward and compensation practices
- Lack of promotions
- Poor equipment
- Hostile employee relationships
- Excellent job market
- Families moving out of the area

Any number of or combination of reasons could be responsible for the high turnover. For these reasons, discovering root cause is essential to long-term problem-solving and sustainable interventions.

Focusing on the areas that pose the most serious threat to the organization or will cause significant harm is not always what was initially requested, but important to the organization's overall health. While a Band-Aid may be necessary for the short term, the long-term fix (root cause) needs to be addressed or little will ultimately change. Also, if you assume that what is often requested is not what is needed, it will force a deeper investigation for causation. Even if what is requested is needed, it is important to look deeper. As a result, connections will be made to other parts of the organization so that solutions are more relevant and supported by others in the organization and have less unintended consequences. Always assume that what is known or in front of you is not the entire story/picture and that awareness alone will encourage further inquiry.

COMMON ROOT CAUSES

When searching for the root cause of any situation or problem, several elements seem to have a high level of occurrence regardless of the observable symptoms. While a few are listed here, your organization may have others or additional common causes for current problems. Any situation that has been problematic for years has its roots in the organization's history and should not be taken at face value or simple cause and effect.

- **Leadership is always a part of the problem.** At a minimum, they were not aware of the problem when they should have been or have tolerated or endured the situation thereby enabling the situation often unconsciously. Sometimes, the fix was worse than enduring the problem, so they consciously let the problem alone until it exacerbated. On the flip side, <u>leadership is also always a part of the solution</u> and needs to be, as they will drive the change by nothing more than the allocation of resources to address the problem.

- **Leadership style is also a frequent root cause.** The top-down model is an authoritarian model and is the cause of many non-trusting policies and work practices as well as performance appraisals and relationship issues. Many times, a person receives a promotion because they are the best technically within their area, but as we all know, a good technician does not necessarily make a good manager or leader.

- **The system, policies, rules, practices, and procedures are supporting the problem.** Remember many of today's problems were yesterday's solutions, so rules and practices were put in place for a reason but are no longer necessary and sometimes even harmful to performance or culture.

- **Structure.** Often it is the organizational design and structure (think organizational chart) that is causing the problem. Silos develop; competition between silos, especially competition for scarce resources, is quite common; and the culture becomes one of competition rather than cooperation.

- **The nature of the business.** The nature of the business may also be a root cause of many of the issues, and this is a difficult one to deal with. The nature of the business is essential due to its relationship to the core purpose for which the company exists. For instance, if you are in the intelligence business, many communications are based on a need-to-know basis and communications difficulties are to be expected. If you are in a creative or innovative business, then any organizational structure or policy that is rigid works against the desired creative environment. If you are in the customer service business, then having a lot of policies that are not customer friendly works against you being successful with your customers.

- **Lack of follow-through.** Starting change initiatives and never following through to completion is a common reason for problems. Many organizations will make attempts at change, whether it is culture, process, structure, business models, etc. And many times, the organization loses momentum, reverts to old practices, and leaves staff feeling like change is not effective. This results in a bias toward the status quo and increased challenge in obtaining buy-in for new change efforts.

Determine root cause by applying the Five Whys technique. There is a reason, maybe multiple reasons why the organization has the current behavior it does. The Five Whys is applied to the below true case.

ROOT CAUSE

According to the Associated Press, in 1989 the National Park Service conducted deterioration studies of both the Lincoln and Jefferson memorials. This story is attributed to the Jefferson memorial and is an example of determining root cause.

Problem
The stones in the Jefferson memorial are deteriorating badly.

Why?
The stones have to be cleaned very frequently.

Why?
Pigeons are leaving too many calling cards.

Why all the pigeons?
They feed on the heavy spider population.

Why are there so many spiders?
They are attracted by a huge moth population.

Why all the moths?
They are attracted by the monument lights during their twilight swarming frenzy.

Solution
Turn on the lights two hours later.

In the case above, had you focused on the deteriorating stones or the cleaning services, you may have spent months and hundreds of thousands of dollars attempting to solve the wrong or a nonexistent problem.

COST OF THE PROBLEM

By defining the specific behaviors and how it is affecting the organization, by determining best estimate on the number of individuals and the amount of time those behaviors are present and identifying a cost estimate on the average amount of compensation those individuals receive, you can generally get a number that approximates what it is costing the organization to do nothing and maintain current operations. The OD practitioner can provide great value in helping executives realize the cost of the problem. By doing this simple cost analysis, the numbers are generally surprisingly high. Many executives may not realize that the cost of maintaining the problem is often far greater than the solution. This is one way to show the return on investment (ROI) for your work and is important for any financial analysis the organization may want or need.

EXAMPLE: DETERMINING COSTS

During a diagnostic assessment, a common complaint was that supervisors/managers were spending too much time in meetings, especially nonproductive meetings. Many managers attended meetings with content that had little to nothing to do with their responsibilities. The company wanted all managers to attend these meetings to improve communications and build relationships (these are all good goals). Some managers simply endured the meetings, others learned to multi-task during the meetings, and some managers rebelled and did not show up. Many meetings were informational, and a simple email or text would have accomplished the same goal.

When we asked the managers how much time was wasted in attending non-productive or non-relevant meetings, the average was two to three hours per day.

Analysis

54	Number of managers and supervisors currently in the organization.
2.5	Average number of hours wasted daily per person
12.5	Average number of hours wasted weekly per person
50	Average number of hours wasted monthly per person
600	Average number of hours wasted yearly per person
40	Average hourly salary based on $80,000 per year and 2,000 working hours
$24,000	Average cost per person wasted yearly in meetings
$1,296,000	Average annual amount of managers/ supervisors' wasted time.

When senior managers see that they waste over one million dollars every year on non-productive meetings, they often get a wakeup call as to what the problem is costing them. The solution rarely costs what tolerating the problem costs.

TURNOVER

Another frequent problem in organizations is the hidden costs of employee turnover. In turnover, there are many costs to consider—

the cost of recruiting and advertising, hiring, onboarding, training and development, and the first six months on the job to really understand the organization. Deloitte (The HR Digest, 2018) puts the average cost of turnover at *one and a half to two times* annual salary and the Center for American Progress (2012), citing their research of eleven papers over fifteen years, indicates that it is 213 percent of their annual salary. In addition to the hard costs, there are other soft costs, such as loss of consistency, customer service, new employee orientation, rebuilding a team's relationships when new members arrive, etc.

Employee turnover is often not seen as a high priority because it is not out-of-pocket dollars being spent. The positions were budgeted for in the annual budget, and money saved by not having a position filled often offsets the additional costs of new hires. Nevertheless, this could be money saved by the organization by having low turnover rates. Certain industries have an incredibly high turnover: over 80 percent for long-distance truck drivers, 42 percent of CNA nursing homes, 73 percent of food service workers. According to an article published by Jonathan Hall and Alan Kreuger (2015), in the Uber rideshare company, 11 percent of their drivers stop driving within a month and 50 percent within one year, and according to SHRM (Bauer, 2010), turnover, in general, can be as high as 50 percent in the first eighteen months.

First impressions are said to be important, and not only does the new employee make an impression on their coworkers, but the company also makes an impression on the new employee. According to an article by Maren Hogan (November 30, 2015), a third of employees knew whether or not they would stay with their company long term after just one week. Therefore, onboarding is so important and yet according to a Gallup poll survey (Wigert and Pendell, 2021), *only 12* percent of the respondents said that their company does a good job with onboarding. There are many areas where the OD practitioner can make a positive difference, and this is just one of them.

DESIGN THE INTERVENTION/TRAINING PROGRAM

Most successful interventions are process-oriented, not event-oriented, i.e., training programs. Listed are a few of the questions to be answered when designing any training program:

- When designing the training, how will senior management support the change/training program and to what level will their involvement be necessary?
- How will ongoing support be accomplished and who will be responsible for it? The ongoing support after the training program is what turns an event into a process.
- Can the program/initiative take place over a series of sessions rather than all at once?
- What principles of adult education will be adhered to?
- How, who, what, when, where will the best delivery of the program/initiative be?
- What are the most important activities that need to be addressed and in what priority?

CAUTION: FLAVOR OF THE MONTH

Clients often want to institute interventions that can be offered to most, or all, of the organization, such as training, assessments, or coaching. These events may offer limited content that will help with challenges; however, these activities often end up producing minimal impact and not producing sustainable changes and, ultimately, end up being flavor of the month. There are three main reasons why programs turn into flavor-of-the-month programs that produce little if any sustainable changes.

1. The initiative does not address the root cause of the problems the organization wants to solve.

2. The initiative is not a holistic or systems approach to change and only deals with a limited scope/problem.
3. There is no internal infrastructure built to carry on the change efforts.

Unfortunately, many organizations in their rush for a quick fix or a belief that they have the right solution implement programs without appropriate support: these are referred to as "flavor-of-the-month initiatives." When this occurs, it hurts the initiative itself and negatively impacts employee attitudes and beliefs about the organization and its ability to change, thus future initiatives become suspect.

CONCLUSION

This chapter discussed change and how an organization may approach it, gain and lose momentum for it, and the role the practitioner has in managing that process. Change is constant, and each client will have unique needs and aspirations during the process. A practitioner will benefit from being open to experiencing the process with each client and supporting their needs in a customized and supportive way. Support includes knowing when to encourage more client ownership, understanding that sometimes the practitioner will be deferred to in leading change, and knowing when it may be time to exit a partnership.

DISCUSSION QUESTIONS

- When planning for change, what are important steps to avoid "flavor of the month" initiatives?
- How can the practitioner help a client overcome resistance to change?
- What are the signs a client is not ready for change and any efforts to change will likely be unsuccessful?

- In what ways can a practitioner encourage ownership of change in an organization?
- What are the clues that the client is or is not ready to change?
- Have you ever encountered wanting something to change more than the client wanted it to change? What was the outcome?
- What is the turnover rate in your organization and is that where you think it should be? Is there any particular group with significantly higher turnover? What might be the cause(s) for that?
- In the senior leadership ranks, who in your organization is your strongest support and biggest detractor? What relationships do you need to work on?
- Which groups, teams, and departments have the highest resistance to change? Why?
- What red lights currently exist within your initiatives or programs?

CHAPTER SIX

Engaging in the OD Process

INTRODUCTION

All organizational change efforts have some sort of a sequence or process even if it is unknown to all. There must be a series of steps that take place. Obviously, those change efforts that follow a proven or well-thought-out process tend to be more successful than those that are randomly implemented. This chapter identifies a well-thought-out process. There are other processes, and what is important is that the OD practitioner follows a process that they know well, are comfortable with, and works. In this chapter, we will cover the phases in OD including contracting, goal setting, the diagnostic phase, using discovery interviews effectively, and reporting the diagnostic findings. Also, we will cover the design process, developing the intervention, delivering the intervention, and having an exit strategy. Evaluation and follow up are also a part of the process. Additionally, we will identify projects gone bad and what do you do when you encounter illegal activities. As noted in earlier chapters, the authors believe there is value in conducting diagnostic activities with the clients but acknowledge that the phases in this chapter overlap and many models and styles of OD can be used during any or all of these phases depending on each client's need.

When conducting an organizational assessment, it is important to systematically evaluate the current state of a system. Models are used to help guide practitioners through the process. There are numerous models outlining the engagement process in organization development work. One model used successfully in the past is the DDDDE (diagnosis, design, develop, deliver, evaluate) model explained below. This model is identical to the instructional design model ADDIE (analysis, design, deliver, implement, evaluate), which demonstrates that the same model can be identified differently and used for different purposes. The model is not as important as the process and the finesse with which it is enacted. Any model that includes the following components will aid the OD practitioner in the assessment process:

- assesses the current and possibly historical situation
- looks at the entire system
- designs interventions tailored to the goals and needs of the organizations
- addresses both systems and behaviors
- competently manages the process throughout the delivery phase
- provides support, follow up, and evaluation at the end.

PHASES IN OD

Contracting

While the contracting phase generally happens before any project work begins, this is also the first diagnostic phase. This phase sets the stage for relationship building, trust building, and communications and is often predictive of the entire process. Much can be learned and established during initial meetings, including the foundation for the practitioner's relationship with the client.

The contracting portion is the phase where expectations get established, roles and responsibilities are identified, and goals and deliverables are decided upon; therefore, it is a critical step to any change initiative. It is essential for every project or consulting assignment to start by establishing a clear contract with the client that contains a specific description of work to be performed, deliverables, results, and timeframe.

During the contracting phase, the practitioner has a very strong negotiating position. The establishment of expectations, roles, resources, timeframes, and outcomes are critical. This phase brings clarity to the entire project and establishes boundaries for both the client and the practitioner. The end of this phase should produce explicit agreement regarding all expectations of both client and practitioner. This could be as formal as a legal contract with an external practitioner or a memorandum of understanding with an internal practitioner.

Practitioners need to be aware of project or scope creep and the taking on of extra assignments which likely will reduce focus and other valuable resources committed to the project. This is an excellent topic for discussion at this phase. Listed below are a few of the questions the practitioner might ask.

Project Scope

- What does the client identify as the major problem or focus effort?
- Is the effort focused or limited to one component of the organization or the whole system?
- How pervasive or limited is the problem?
- What previous efforts has the organization engaged in to address the problem?
- How ready for change is the organization?
- How many people will be affected by this effort?
- If the scope changes during the effort, how will those changes be handled?

Project Timeline

- How long does the client expect this effort to take?
- What is a realistic amount of time to engage in the OD process?
- If the effort is not achievable in the client's timeframe, how can scaling the scope or process help to make incremental progress in the expected timeframes?
- How long will each phase of the process take based on the scope?

Resources

- Have sufficient resources space, materials, equipment, people, and finances been dedicated to this project?
- If additional resources are necessary, what is the process for obtaining them, and who makes the decisions?
- Will the client dedicate internal staff to this project? If so, who manages them?
- How much travel will be required?

Expected Outcomes

- What is the exit/completion point?
- What are the milestones to deliver to the client stakeholders?
- What is the expected outcome of the project?
- Are there incremental deliverables expected? What are they and when are they due?

Key Partners and Stakeholders

- Are 80 percent of leadership on board with a change effort?
  - Who is not on board?
  - Why are they not on board?

- o   What does that person need to become a supporter?
- o   Who will work with that (those) person(s)?
- o   What are the risks for proceeding without that person being on board?
- o   Does this stop the project?

- Are there internal resources available for support throughout the project?
- Who will support the effort in the organization once the partnership/project/contract ends?
- What are the roles and expectations for key contributors, including the practitioner?

"WHO IS THE CLIENT?"

This is a critical question to get clarity on regardless of whether you are an internal or external practitioner. The organization is always the client, not the person that hires you. The person that hires you may be part of the problem and could potentially be the main problem. Therefore, it is critical to establish an agreement on your role in the organization and who the client is. It is also important that the client understands that any recommendations you will make, or advice you will give, will be in the best interest of the organization and not necessarily in the best interest of a limited group of client members or the individual.

Also, the person who hires you may not be in a position of influencing the organization's engagement in activities, change, or outcome of any effort. The initial contact for a project may be seeking your assistance as an OD practitioner to convince leaders of the importance of a change effort. It is important to be aware of the level of influence your point of contact has so that you know how to best support both your contact and the broader initiative. Sometimes, your contacts will remain the point of contact who brought you in, but your true influencers of change are other leaders within the organization. It is helpful to use the contracting phase to start determining who will be most supportive of and influential in a change effort.

While the contracting phase generally happens before any project work begins, this is also the first diagnostic phase. This phase sets the stage for relationship building, trust building, and communications and is often predictive of the entire process. Much can be learned and established during initial meetings, including the foundation for the practitioner's relationship with the client.

The contracting phase is an excellent time to assess the possibility of success or failure. There are projects that are set up to fail from the beginning (discussed elsewhere in the book), and it is during this contracting phase that it would be beneficial for all parties to discover if this is the case. Characteristics of projects being set up for failure include clients who are unrealistic about expectations or who already have an answer or solution to their perceived problems. If during initial conversations the practitioner senses the project will be a waste of time or money, or will not solve the problem, then it is important to bring the issues to the table for discussion. A best practice is not to agree to an effort that is not attainable.

Goal Setting

The goal(s) for the intervention should be established during the initial contracting phase. The OD practitioner is encouraged to develop a list of organization-specific questions they may want to ask during the contracting phase to both determine and encourage clearly established project goals:

- What would success look like?
- What do you need to see when this work is finished?
- What is it costing you if the problem is not solved?
- What specific behaviors do you want to see more/less of?
- If we are successful in this initiative, how will this affect the organization?

- If we are not successful in this initiative, how will this affect the organization?
- What is your expectation of time and when this might be completed?
- Who will need to be involved?
- Who do I report to?

The OD practitioner should know what is expected of them and determine if the resources and timelines reasonably support attainment. The OD practitioner will likely need to be flexible in the process and decide where to adjust to meaningfully help the client. Many clients will want to engage in a process that is action-oriented and will be tempted to skip all phases of a diagnostic. A practitioner will want to emphasize the importance of a diagnostic, but also be able to scale these services in a way that leads to intervention in an efficient way. Consider the minimum amount of diagnostic activity required to determine interventions. Also consider if there are any short-term interventions that can occur before the diagnosis is complete. Doing this may help gain momentum and energy for the larger, long-term interventions.

Another key question to consider is, "What is the business case for this work?" It is important to understand what the client expects to be different when the work is completed, the ideal result. Helping the client identify the business case, the problems, and their cost to the organization helps in identifying the return on investment (ROI), which is critical if the organization is going to invest significant dollars in corrective actions. Often in the initial stages, the work requested does not identify nor address the root cause and usually is either addressing a symptom of the organization or requested solution, i.e., we have low morale (symptom) and need a motivational speaker (solution) or we do not cooperate very well (symptom) and need a team-building program (solution). For these reasons, part of the initial contract may be an assessment of current conditions (diagnostic) to ensure that you are addressing a real problem and its cause.

DIAGNOSTIC

As discussed in the contracting phase, an OD practitioner will likely need to spend time gaining an understanding of the current climate and situation. Several outcomes are a part of the diagnostic phase:

- Define the problem, make sure there is a problem, and if so, identify root cause(s).
- Identify and define potential solution(s).
- Identify or describe what will be different when the situation is corrected.

The diagnostic phase involves designing a structured approach to gathering information that helps the practitioner understand the root causes and the current state of the climate and culture. Structured does not mean rigid. Data can be obtained via a variety of measures such as surveys, interviews, storytelling, focus groups, and reviewing existing human capital data (such as turnover rates, exit survey information, or grievances). Another part of the process involves understanding what the company currently spends on the problem and what they could save if the problem were corrected. Identify the behaviors and put a cost estimate on each.

Data Gathering

Every contact with the client is a chance to collect additional data to help refine the picture of the people, process, and organization. Data analysis is best done by two or more practitioners to avoid single-person bias and increase problem-solving options. This may include a grouping of issues, systems review, priority setting, and root cause analysis. This phase can be considered as a part of the diagnosis phase or the beginning of the design phase.

Discovery Interviews

A discovery interview is a powerful tool that every OD practitioner would benefit from learning. Not only is it highly effective in uncovering information, but it helps build relationships, ensures understanding, builds lines of communication, and shows compassion. It is both a skill and an art to use this process effectively and effortlessly. One of the key benefits is that it helps you discover information that would not have been discovered with a rigid interview format. It allows you to follow the thoughts of the speaker rather than direct the speaker's thinking. In a rigid format or a fixed set of questions, you only get answers to the questions asked, and if you ask the wrong questions, you tend to get the wrong answers.

EXAMPLE

Years ago, a car rental company was pushing customer service so every time you rented a car from them, they would ask you how their customer service was. I never had a bad customer service experience with them as they were always polite, friendly, and knowledgeable. I did have a few bad car rental experiences, but they never knew it because they asked the wrong question. All they ever asked about was their customer service, not their car rental experience. They never once asked me how the car was or if I had any problems. Had they done so, they would have received different feedback and would have been more informed as to how they were doing as a car rental company.

As seen in the car rental example, rigid, fixed question interviews limit the information you might receive from the questions asked. Generally, a discovery process will follow the thinking of the respondent; however, it may be beneficial to have a fixed set of open-ended questions (i.e., What is it like to work here?) in the instance that conversation stalls or to provoke additional thoughts.

Here is an example of the discovery interview process. The interviewer might begin with a general or focused open-ended question—"Tell me about your work experience here?"—and the respondent might say something like, "Well, lately, it has been very frustrating because of the inefficiencies and duplication of efforts. No one seems to know what is going on here." That response just brought up many avenues for potential exploration.

- Timeframe: Lately
- Frustrations: Emotions
- Process: Inefficiencies
- Process/Resources: Duplication of effort
- Leadership: No one/bosses

Any of these areas is an opportunity to explore further, and some questions that could be used are as follows:

- What were things like before now?
- What is contributing to the fact that no one seems to know what is going on here?
- Is it everyone that does not know what is going on or just a few key individuals?
- How come no one seems to know what is going on here?
- What would have to change for people to know what is going on here?
- Tell me more about...
- When you say . . . (frustrating), what do you mean?
- Can you give me an example of . . . ? (inefficiencies)

Essentially, the discovery process follows the thoughts of the speaker, capitalizing on their responses to dig deeper into the areas that they bring up. You follow their train of thought until that avenue dries up and then redirect them back to another avenue that they either brought up or that you feel needs to be covered. The discovery interview process is a powerful tool.

People as Symptoms

People reflect both the policies and practices of the organization, as well as the climate and culture of the organization. The OD practitioner merely needs to look at the health of the relationships to gain a perspective of the health of the organization. Another valuable service the OD practitioner can offer their client is to look at the health factor of the individuals as well. Here are a few areas the practitioner might consider:

- Sleep: Does the organization encourage a culture of hard work, little sleep? Are people routinely working overtime? Poor sleep has been associated with less employee engagement, creativity, innovation, efficiency, and productivity (Walker, 2017).

- Alcohol or drug use: Are after-work trips to the local watering hole encouraged? Are a lot of parties encouraged?

- Physical ailments and sick time: Do people frequently take all of their allotted sick time whether they are sick or not?

- Work-related injuries/Workman's compensation claims: Is there a high incident of injuries, and if so, in what areas?

- Workplace violence: Is the environment physically safe? Are there security measures in place?

- Obesity: What percentage of the workforce is unhealthy due to obesity?

- Disease incidents: Is there a higher rate of certain disease, i.e., cancer in a chemical plant?

Any organization that is not physically and mentally healthy will have a more difficult time competing with those that are.

REPORTING DIAGNOSTIC RESULTS

As a result of diagnostic efforts, a practitioner will be expected to provide their findings to the client. The practitioner needs to remember their neutral and objective position in this process. The practitioner's interpretation, understanding, and ability to present the data in a manner that clearly outlines an organization's current state is critical. It may be tempting to remove information that may be unfavorable, but it would be a disservice to clients to do so. The practitioner's role is to speak truth to power, and providing the full findings of a diagnostic is one of the most powerful steps in any intervention. How can any organization expect to change if the full reality of its current state remains unknown after a diagnostic?

In addition, it would be unwise to assume that the report will be welcomed, even if it is anxiously awaited and often requested. Shedding light on the organizational problems, even if already known, is not always welcomed. There is something about how now that the problems are in writing and not just hallway talk makes them real. Now the problems will have to be dealt with, and what if a major part of the problem is those receiving the report? Both candidness and diplomacy are in order here, and it may be that pre-report work, visiting one on one with various individuals, is necessary before the group report. We have seen examples of an external consultant has withheld difficult information in order not to alienate the client. The failure to provide honest feedback limits what the client is aware of, will work on, and will achieve.

For this reason, report writing is critical. Reports can generally follow a format with these major sections:

- Background/Purpose
- Process/Methodology
- Findings/Recommendations

The beginning of the report should include the process of information collecting, those involved, timeframe, and other appropriate methodological or process information. Following this are the findings and recommendations. At this point, an important consideration is what to include without violating any confidentiality agreements. Also, writing involves a balance of diplomacy and candidness to be both candid about the problems and the severity of their impact. In general, direct quotes are far more powerful than summary data. When including a direct quote, as a rule of thumb, no names should be identified with the quote; rather, identify departments or areas where the quotes originate if the origin is necessary at all.

The report is a powerful document. It puts into writing the existing issues, both previously known and unknown within the organization, and the recommendations for improvements. It is no longer hearsay or rumors but is now documented. For many organizations, this is a major wake-up call. This is often used as a living document or a part of their strategic planning for years to come. The report ideally will be both a source of motivation and a call to action. Listed below are a few tips for report writing.

- Logistics

  - A time frame of the data collection
  - Groups or number of individuals involved in the data collection
  - Names of those collecting the data consultants, researchers
  - Methods used, i.e., interviews, focus groups, surveys, observation, etc.
  - Locations involved

- Findings

  o Themes
  o Direct quotes
  o Case examples
  o Charts or graphs
  o Organizational impact descriptions

- Recommendations

  o Critical first steps
  o Longer improvements

It is advisable that reports include a clear statement indicating that while recommendations are made, it is the responsibility of the client organization to accept, alter, or decline those recommendations. The practitioner can anticipate that some of their recommendations will not be accepted or followed even if accepted. Very few companies follow all the recommendations of any practitioner.

The final action in this phase is to deliver the report to senior leaders for their review and action planning. A best practice in the diagnostic phase is to include a senior management meeting to discuss the report, the findings, and recommendations. This part is critical in that it encourages senior leaders to own the information and plan the next steps toward implementation and organizational improvement. A comprehensive approach to planning includes identifying dedicated resources (financial, human resource, and material) along with timeframes, responsible parties, monitoring, progress reporting, etc. At least 80 percent of all senior leaders (the critical mass) need to agree and be supportive of the change initiative. If they are not in agreement with the practitioner's report, what will they do to improve the organization?

Delivering the report can be said to be the end of the diagnostic phase or the beginning of the design or delivery phase or all the phases. The DDDDE model is very fluid and was never intended to be a linear process.

DESIGN

Once the diagnostic phase is complete and data has been analyzed, the next phase involves designing interventions to address the concerns or make improvements within the organization. Often there are many areas of improvement that can be addressed, and there is a priority beginning with those that either have the greatest payoff or have severe and immediate consequences to the organization if not addressed. Interventions can include almost any improvement initiative. Listed are a few of the more common interventions:

- Policy and work practices reviews
- Rules and regulations
- Organization design
- Cultural change
- Development of mission, vision, and values
- Human capital management issues
- Customer service issues
- Quality and performance improvement issues
- Training and development of staff
- Conflict resolution

What to address and when is a question of priorities and can be used in the design, development, or delivery stages. Two well-established resources for guiding priorities include those of Alex MacKenzie and Steven Covey. Alex MacKenzie's book, *The Time Trap* (1975), and Stephen Covey's *The 7 Habits of Highly Effective People* (2004), first published in 1989, both identified the same matrix with MacKenzie focusing on task and Covey focusing on personal goals.

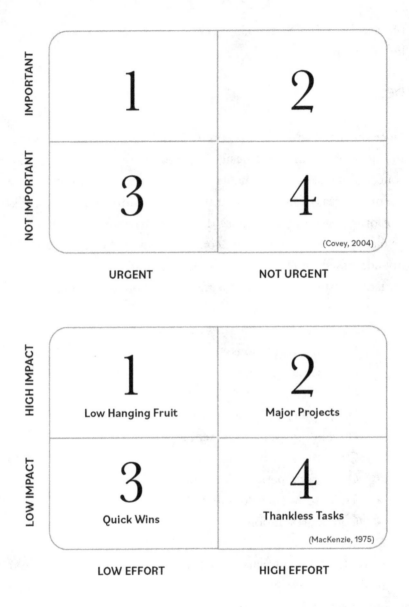

In the MacKenzie quadrangle, the focus should be on those projects that require little effort but produce high impact first and then a balance for high impact, high effort and low impact, low effort but avoiding high effort, low impact work. In the Covey quadrangle, the focus should be in quadrant one and two on the important items regardless of urgency, although for many of us the urgent takes priority over the important until they themselves become urgent. Both models offer an excellent way to determine in the design phase what work should have the highest priority. There are times, however, when the practitioner is asked to implement a predetermined solution. Immediate questions to ask include the following:

- What benefit will this provide the organization?
- Is this solution addressing the root cause or just addressing the symptoms?
- Is this solution the entire solution or only a part of the solution?
- What potential unintended consequences might this solution have?
- Have those individuals who will be affected by the solution been involved in choosing the solution?

A frequent request by client organizations is training programs. While training programs have their place and are an important part of many change initiatives, they are not the answer to everything. Training programs are very appropriate when there are knowledge or skill issues, but not as appropriate when there are behavioral issues. Training programs are usually events, while organizational change is usually a process.

Listed here are a few of the design elements for large-scale change that may need to be considered in the design phase.

- Is this a reactive engagement (problem-or deficiency-centered issue) or a proactive engagement (future- or benefit-oriented)?
- What work processes need to be changed to improve efficiency, quality, customer service, or production?
- What policies need to be changed to improve efficiency, quality, customer service, or production?

- Does the leadership style need to change and, if so, from what to what?
- Does the organization have a clearly defined mission, vision, and values statement that employees embrace?
- What factors support or will work against the initiative?
- What is the level of resistance to change?
- Who will be your greatest supporters/resistors?
- What time constraints will you have?
- Prioritize the implementation steps.
- Who will oversee the project?
- Who will be responsible for implementation?
- How will the program/initiative be evaluated?
- What employees need to be involved/trained?
- What deliverables are expected and by when?

The OD practitioner may want to advise a client where they could reasonably start and make a positive impact. Perhaps a starting point would be facilitated discussions with some leaders, and once these leaders are functioning better, then other organizational initiatives can begin. A practitioner should be able to scale initiatives and services to help a client navigate the complexity of their own issues and needs. While we would all like to help make large-scale change that positively impacts a whole organization, often we will have to accept that funding, organizational dynamics, leader decisions, etc. will influence exactly what work we can engage in at any moment in time.

In a large-scale project, there are often many starting points, and the OD practitioner may need to facilitate a meeting with the senior leaders to gain consensus on which activities might have the greatest impact and establish the priorities. It is not uncommon that the starting point is with the senior leadership team or some portion thereof. There will be times when the issues are many but time, people, or budgets do not support doing everything, and the OD practitioner will need to scale the initiatives and services to have the greatest impact while fitting into the organizational constraints. There may be times when the constraints are so restrictive that *not* proceeding is the best course of action. In these cases, the OD practitioner will have the often-difficult task of speaking truth to power and advising the client of the same or accepting the constraints and advising the client of what limited impact can be expected under these conditions.

The practitioner can expect that once the design is finished, it will probably change many times before the project is completed, and it sometimes changes before the implementation begins. This is normal, as new information becomes available (including new priorities) and new needs become identified. Design is always based on the information available at the time, considering the anticipated impact on the entire system and any potential unintended consequences. A part of the reason the design phase can frequently change is that the environment and information change rapidly. Many mid-implementation changes (course corrections) are common. Ultimately, it is extremely rare that the implementation goes completely according to plan. The OD practitioner's flexibility is key to success both in the design and delivery.

DEVELOP

Much of the development of a change initiative is already accomplished in the design phase; however, many of the logistics are not. Design can be the view from 30,000 feet and the development phase can be all the work that needs to take place before you take off and for the first 10,000 feet. Development includes the planning of the programs, tasks, and resources that will be a part of the change process. Development can be the writing or planning for a simple singular task or a complex set of interrelated programs and tasks. Here are a few of the considerations:

- Will coaching be a part of this initiative?
- Will conflict resolution be a part of this initiative?

- What groups and/or departments will be involved?
- How many employees will be involved?
- Will these initiatives require discussion groups and problem-solving teams?
- Who will be the responsible individuals for each initiative?
- What is the timeframe for each initiative?
- How will senior leadership be involved?
- What resources will be required?
- What external support/consultants/trainers will be required?
- What other internal resources are required (i.e., budget, human resources, training and development) to determine cost, scope, etc.?
- What are short-term and long-term priorities?
- How will this initiative be communicated and by whom?
- Will training and development be a part of this initiative? If training is to be included once again, there are many questions:

  ○ Do we purchase an existing off-the-shelf program or develop our own internal program?
  ○ Who will deliver the program, internal personnel, or contractors?

- Who will attend the program, and will attendance be mandatory, recommended, or voluntary?
- Will this be individually attended, or will it be taught to entire workgroups?
- What are the desired takeaways from this program, thinking differently, feeling differently, or behaving differently?
- When is the training to take place in the change process?

DELIVERY

Once implementation plans are in place, the practitioner moves to deliver these activities. However, any time the OD practitioner is in the delivery phase, they are also continuing in the diagnostic phase. Diagnosis is a never-ending process, and the OD practitioner is constantly collecting information that may alter current plans (design phase). Working with staff at all levels in the organization on a task is a very natural and less obvious way to collect information. Group dynamics, communications, attitudes, and leadership style, levels of resistance or acceptance are among the many bits of information that are readily available when working together on an initiative.

When in the delivery phase, it is important to consider that delivery of a single initiative is more straightforward than delivery across an entire system, which is far more complex, time-consuming, and interconnected. These complex initiatives often require many simultaneous projects and many facilitators, both internal and external. Managing these projects and all the different relationships therein is an important and time-consuming part of the OD practitioner's responsibility. High-maintenance clients require a lot of handholding, and decreasing their dependence on the practitioner will be a more difficult but necessary task.

It is a best practice to maximize delivery using internal resources at the client organization whenever possible. Staff involvement is important for commitment and ownership of the process. The OD practitioner might well consider being the conductor rather than a member of the band. It is especially important for the external practitioner to begin immediately decreasing the organization's dependence on them and increasing the organization's capability to be independent and self-managing. Developing an internal infrastructure to implement the change and to carry on (follow up) long after the OD practitioner is gone is also important. This will add to the sustainability of any project.

Developing an internal infrastructure can take on many forms from the simple to the complex. Essentially it is getting those who will be affected by the change, involved in managing and delivering the changes. It is transferring ownership of the project and process to the employees. The OD practitioner then becomes the conductor/advisor and not the implementer. This work typically involves employees working on various committees, providing training to others, problem-solving and strategic planning groups, and project oversight and management. There will be an identified owner or person responsible for the ongoing support and continuation of the project. This person(s) will be responsible for future results.

PROJECT COMPLETION. EXIT POINT.

"Begin with the end in mind" was Stephen Covey's second habit in his book *The 7 Habits of Highly Effective People* (2004). When do you declare victory and walk away? What does success look like? What are the deliverables and what takes place once they are delivered? What follow up would be beneficial and by whom? How will the program results be evaluated? When and how does your responsibility end? These are a few of the questions that would be beneficial to define during the contracting phase. Having a clear ending point, in addition to set mutual expectations, tends to guard against project and scope creep. If the endpoint is clearly identified, then any project or scope changes would involve a reallocation of resources and time expectations.

A practitioner will need to be well versed in creating a manageable approach to any change initiative. Developing the approach includes developing the exit strategy, and while dates and times will likely change, the deliverables or the results generally do not.

FOLLOW-UP AND EVALUATION

While the phases are presented linearly in this book, in practice, they are fluid and interconnected with every step in the process. Evaluation not only assesses the effectiveness of the effort, the ROI, but the unintended consequences as well. Constant evaluation leads to new diagnostics, planning, and delivery. Program evaluations can show problems, identify performance improvements, enhance customer service, and validate both the initiative and the practitioner. If the problems and their impact/costs were clearly identified during the diagnostic phase, then demonstrating performance improvements should be relatively easy.

So much of what is asked for and what is implemented by an OD practitioner is difficult to measure. If an organization asks for a training program, we can easily count the number of people who attended the program, look at the materials each student was provided, and get some statistics from the evaluation sheets provided by the students at the end of the program. However, if the practitioner implements a cultural change initiative and helps the culture change from a predominantly negative and conflictual culture to a more positive and collaborative culture, it is much more difficult to measure the effectiveness of the effort. It is often easier to measure the output than the input. If you consider that organizations only change when the people in them change, then the OD practitioner is in the business of changing people so that the organization itself can change. People change is difficult to measure. How do you measure someone's attitude improvement other than self-reporting or peer observation? There are hard numbers that can generally be obtained:

- Employee turnover
- Accident rate
- Employee/union grievances
- Customer complaints

- Lawsuits
- Profitability
- Quality output/defects
- Overtime compensation, etc.

These numbers represent the symptom and not the cause; they represent human behavior, not the instigator. Nevertheless, they are often numbers that are available. More difficult to assess is the effect of a policy or procedure change or a position change, or the effect of leadership training on the workforce. How do you measure the effect of a more positive working atmosphere or the impact due to the organization now focusing more on strategic human capital management? There are jobs emerging in the field of "people analytics." These professionals are focused on obtaining, producing, and analyzing human capital data so that organizations can make strategic decisions. Specialists in analytics will help identify methods and data that can answer diagnostic questions posed by OD, locate or generate data as needed, analyze and develop insights based on data, take action, and measure effectiveness. By leveraging analytics professionals, OD practitioners may have increased access to data that helps measure the state of an organization and the results of interventions.

It is rarely a single initiative that significantly changes one of the hard numbers like employee turnover. Generally, there is a combination of causes contributing to the problem. Even if there is one main cause, by the time that cause has changed substantially, and the employees begin to trust that the change will be sustained, it could be long after the initiative has been completed and the change would not necessarily be attributed to the initial effort.

EVALUATING DIFFERENT ORGANIZATIONS

There are some organizations that do not care about evaluations and proof that the effort was worthwhile. There are some organizations that are adamant about evaluations and do an excellent job of measurement. There are also organizations that are overly concerned with metrics, outputs, evidence-based results, charting, project management, etc. (all the mechanicals) when they might be better off being concerned about employee energy, creativity, innovation, engagement, and the entire organizational culture. There are organizations that say they want the evaluations, but by the time the initiative is over, one or more events happen to cause them to move on without the evaluations or with minimal evaluations. Causes of this include the following:

- They decide that determining the return on investment (Kilpatrick's level four [Kirkpatrick, 1994]) is too costly. They have seen sufficient proof along the way and feel they do not need any more proof.
- By the time the evaluation is due, they need the OD resources elsewhere to deal with current problems.

Anytime the OD practitioner conducts an evaluation, that is another chance for additional diagnostic information and the evaluation itself is another chance for implementation and change. Remember, the evaluation itself is an intervention.

Projects Gone Bad

What about projects gone bad? Is there an exit strategy/agreement? If during the diagnostic phase (or at any time), various discoveries or new information become available that indicate the project is doomed to failure or can never succeed, how is this handled? Sometimes the project starts out perfectly fine, but then other legitimate crises occur, draining valuable resources from your initiative, rendering it all but dead. Sometimes it is the introduction of a new boss or the acquisition of additional responsibilities or a major customer or environmental change that dictates changes to the very nature and scope of a project. Are the new conditions acceptable to you? Can you succeed under the new conditions?

Some projects are doomed before they begin, such as poorly designed efforts, lack of funding, only doing the project to meet a minimum legal requirement, the pet project of someone who is due to leave shortly, an organization near bankruptcy and this is a last-ditch effort to survive, etc. Many times, either the budget or time constraints will limit the scope of the project. Are those limitations realistic? Sometimes the scope of the project is so limited that the end is obvious—i.e., delivering a two-day team-building program to operations—and at other times there is no end in sight as in a cultural change initiative. Sometimes the end is not obvious but necessary, and a selected date then serves as either a changeable goal or a cutoff point.

There are many times when there are unrealistic conditions or expectations attached to a project with insufficient resources and they desire miracles for outcomes. Being mindful and refusing to enter into these projects under the current conditions may be both wise and necessary. When these limiting or disastrous conditions are present, it is important to let the client know. Also, what are your recommendations for the client? If you are an internal OD professional and the organization insists, then you may have a number of tough decisions you will need to make, including personal ones.

Is there a difference between an internal and external OD consultant need for an ending point, and if so, what is that difference? The internal consultant may have the luxury of not having to worry as much about the ending point since their projects can take a little longer due to other position responsibilities and they may not have to worry as much about building an internal infrastructure to support the changes since they themselves can provide the support. There is still a need for an agreed-upon ending point. Whether you are internal or external, the goal should always be to help the team, department, or organization be independent of your support, to develop and mature as a team/department/organization.

ILLEGAL ACTIVITIES

During any diagnostic or discovery process, it is not uncommon that the practitioner may encounter activities or behavior that are either illegal or border on illegal. What is the obligation of the practitioner? Are the obligations different for an internal versus external practitioner? What about behaviors that are not illegal but may be immoral or unethical? What are the OD practitioner's responsibilities in these circumstances? There is a sparsity of guidelines for the OD practitioner regarding these issues.

There are both state and federal laws to consider or country laws for international practitioners. In addition, the organization may have policies or regulations that must be followed, and there may even be contract considerations for the external practitioner. While reporting perceived illegal activities has its own risk, non-reporting has its risk as well. Being complicit in illegal activities is not something any practitioner would want. In addition to the law, the practitioner may choose to identify which of their personal values are being violated. Both the laws and one's personal values can act as a guideline in these situations. Prior to reporting any perceived illegal activities, these steps might act as a guideline:

- Be sure of the facts. Hearsay or other people's reporting are not facts unless you have that person's written, signed statement.
- Document everything you know to be factual.
- Determine seriousness. Egregious crimes, robbery, physical or sexual abuse, homicides, etc. will need to be reported to a policing agency, while less serious crimes may need to be reported to the organization first.
- If internal reporting, report your findings to your internal supervisor or point of contact for external consultants.

A guide for immoral or unethical issues would once again be the corporate policies and the practitioner's values and any professional guidelines or code of conduct obligations. There will be consequences when reporting such activities, including loss of trust, being labeled a snitch or untrustworthy, being subsequently rendered ineffective in future work, and even loss of a job. There also may be positive consequences, such as increased trust and stature. In the final analysis, the practitioner must know that the course of action they chose is in alignment with their values and who they are as a practitioner.

CONSULTING ELEMENTS

In this section, we address a number of elements, conditions, and activities that affect the practitioner's role, including types of thinking that affect problem-solving, unintended consequences of implementation, the importance of building relationships, leadership's role in building relationships, assessing and building trust, team building, group dynamics, the practitioners role in the organization, training and development initiatives, as well as developing the necessary infrastructure to enable programs to continue.

PROBLEM-SOLVING AND DECISION-MAKING

If an organization is a living, interconnected ecosystem, then it stands to reason that no problem nor solution is a standalone event. Often, however, organizations look at a problem with a singular focus and do not see the interconnectedness to the rest of the organization. Listed below are three very different mindsets that people often have when viewing a problem. There is no one correct mindset, and each can be appropriate depending on the desired outcome.

Simple–Stopgap

Systemic–Corrective

Strategic–Preventive

Simple solutions tend to be a Band-Aid fix. It is simple cause and effect. These solutions have an immediate focus—fix the current problem. These can be appropriate fixes, especially during a crisis. They are usually, however, a temporary fix limited in scope.

Systemic solutions tend to find and address root causes and usually are permanent fixes. Corrective action is taken not only on the problem itself but also on those conditions or elements that caused the problem.

Strategic solutions are those that are developed by looking ahead at what problems might develop and then preventing them from developing in the first place.

UNINTENDED CONSEQUENCES

There are consequences to every action and every nonaction. It is extremely rare that all the consequences of any change initiative are known prior to implementation. It may be wise to assume that there will always be unintended consequences. Sometimes the unintended consequences are small and hardly noticeable, while at other times they are significant, difficult to fix, and showstoppers.

Unintended consequences are issues that were not foreseen and not planned or anticipated. Without thorough planning, they are often difficult to uncover prior to implementation. Many change initiatives are driven by a singular driving force, such as saving money or increasing profitability or improving customer service, or efficiency and quality. Sometimes the change does accomplish its singular goal but causes numerous other problems in other areas, and sometimes it does not accomplish its singular goal because of all the other problems the change caused. This approach is often associated with simple solutions (cause and effect).

One of the reasons that unintended consequences happen is that those who will be directly involved in the change are not involved in the planning; they were not given a voice. If those who are responsible for implementing the changes or will be impacted by the changes are not involved in the early discussions, it is easy to miss the nuances and subtleties of their work that will be affected by the changes until it is too late. As a rule of thumb, the further those who are designing the change are from the area of change, the more unintended consequences.

Another reason that unintended consequences occur is that those designing the change are not seeing the impact of those changes on all other elements of the organization (system). They are focusing myopically on a limited area(s) and not seeing the interconnectability. Again, maybe all the right people are not involved in the planning.

Still, another reason for unintended consequences is the sense of urgency to implement. Being under extreme time pressure to implement is a recipe for missing many details, some of which may be significant.

RELATIONSHIPS

The OD practitioner, whether internal or external, must build and maintain healthy, positive, trusting relationships with all stakeholders at all levels throughout the organization. The significance, nor the difficulty, of this cannot be understated. It may well be the most important task the practitioner must do. Further, the maintenance of healthy relationships often requires more effort and time than the initial establishment of those relationships. All work gets done through relationships, so the belief in the OD practitioner and the authority or intelligence ascribed to the practitioner in a large part depends on the relationship employees and clients have with the OD practitioner. Building relationships becomes even more challenging with remote workers who can easily live in different parts of the world and who may never have been or will be at the company's physical location.

Since organizational performance may at least in part depend on interpersonal relationships, the belief in the OD practitioner and building a positive relationship with employees is critical and depends on many factors, including trust, intent, authority, knowledge, and skills. Building relationships with everyone is difficult and in some cases cannot be done at all. For instance, how do you build a relationship that is positive and trusting with someone that is not trustworthy, does not have the same values as you, cheats, lies, and is a bully, contentious, and toxic? How do you work with people who think the whole world should revolve around them, are megalomaniacs, and have big egos, treat people as beneath themselves, or work with people who are argumentative, incendiary, blaming, and otherwise negative and conflictual? Worse still, how do you work with people who might be creating a hostile work environment, biased, sexually harassing, stealing or otherwise doing illegal activities? Stay long enough in the field of OD and you may well run into all these types.

Building a positive relationship with someone who is toxic may not be possible and at the very least extremely difficult and time-consuming. In these cases, the OD practitioner has limited choices and a difficult decision to make. The choices include the following:

- Refuse the assignment.
- Attempt to work around the individual.
- Find some small area of agreement or common ground and work on that area (limited engagement).
- Have others work with that individual.

While none of these options are ideal, it may be the reality.

LEVELS OF RELATIONSHIPS

Undoubtedly there are many ways to describe the levels of closeness and connection in relationships. When observing high-performance groups, they cluster around the higher levels of trust, caring, and collaboration in their relationships. It is difficult to imagine a high-performance organization that is filled with conflict and acrimony and little trust. The following is offered as one model or way to gauge relationships.

- **Highly conflicted environment.** Open conflict, low or no trust, frequent arguments, or disagreements, highly negative verbiage and thought processes, employee complaints, union grievances, lawsuits, vindictiveness, revenge, physical and emotional safety concerns.

- **Negative environment.** People put their head down and keep to their own, closed doors, backstabbing conversations, pessimistic, cynical, skeptical, outlooks. Work is just a means to an end; their life and many of their thoughts are elsewhere. Characterized by low trust and fearful attitude.

- **Surface harmony environment.** Cordial, and even at times, interested. Go along to get along attitude, low levels of conflict and candidness. Work reasonably well together and in a crisis work even better together, little conflict but no strong bond either. A tendency to avoid conflict and interpersonal closeness.

- **Positive environment.** Higher levels of trust, candid and open conversation, respectful, yet candid. Healthy conflict that focuses on the issues, not the person. A willingness for activities outside of work together. Celebrations are common. Enjoyment of each other's company.

- **Caring environment.** Pervasive high trust and open communication. A true respect and caring for one another. Highly supportive, share common goals and values. High willingness to give one another feedback in non-threatening ways. Knowing one another beyond surface knowledge. Knowing that you are supported by teammates.

Many teams operate at a surface harmony level and are perfectly content with that level of closeness and do not want to invest the time and energy to get any closer. For those individuals who are at a job, this level of closeness is often considered good. For those individuals who are passionate about what they do or their organization, surface harmony seems to leave something missing or wanting. They tend to seek stronger relationships. The OD consultant can gain great insights into the culture of an organization by merely observing the level of relationships most employees have in the organization.

LEADERSHIP IS ABOUT RELATIONSHIP

For over sixty years, numerous authors have embraced and argued for the importance of relationships within leadership. People do not voluntarily follow someone they do not trust or have a good relationship with. Followership depends on the relationship, and you cannot be a leader unless you have followers. Here are some examples of the leadership theories that discuss the importance of relationships:

- Douglas McGregor in 1950 created Theory X and Y styles of leadership, people versus task styles of leadership.
- Dansereau, Graen, and Haga's (1975) work on LMX Leader-Member Exchange, derived from their transformational leadership approach, states that all people tend to have

an in-group of associates you would rather spend time with and an out-group you would not choose to spend time with. The research states that either consciously or unconsciously you treat these groups differently.

- Bernard Bass (1978) talked about his four *Is*— idealized influence, inspirational motivation, individual consideration, and intellectual stimulation. All four are building blocks to strong relationships.
- Kouzes & Posner (2017) wrote about facilitating relationships.
- Blanchard and Broadwell (2018) wrote about servant leadership in action, and there have been dozens of others.

How do you get dedicated, engaged, loyal, creative, innovative passionate employees if you do not have positive, trusting relationships? How do you build a great place to work without positive, trusting relationships?

With more and more remote and off-site employees, freelancers, and contractors, there is more isolation and less social contact. Since most human beings tend to be social animals, this can be problematic. Today there are productivity sites, motivational sites, work clubs, coworking groups all online, and dozens of apps you can use to help you stay motivated and focused. These sites state that participants are better able to stay focused, have mutual task reinforcement, and positive peer pressure. So instead of being alone and no one is watching, you are in a group with everyone watching, public accountability.

Today, you can hop on your stationary bike and exercise with people from all around the world whom you never met nor ever will. You can live in a virtual world to build your own imaginary cities, cars, apartments, and even sex partners. You can watch anime and sci-fi pictures all day long and never be in reality. You can turn people off at the flick of a switch, block people from sending you stuff, defriend people and take them off of your settings, etc. How is this affecting relationships, our ability to be intimate, deal with conflict, handle personality differences, etc.?

One way to look at relationships is to look at the levels of relationships that affect culture, productivity, and performance. Bruce Tuckman (1965) identified four stages of group development—Forming, Storming, Norming, and Performing—and these continue to have relevance to this day.

TRUST

Trust is necessary, not optional, for all good, sustained relationships. Trust is necessary for organizations to be considered high performing. When trust levels throughout the organization are high, the cost of operations goes down and quality, customer service, and productivity go up. Conversely, when trust is low, the reverse happens: operational costs go up and quality, customer service, and productivity go down (Covey, 2008). Trust is a critical and essential factor in building a productive and high-performing culture and in building positive relationships.

According to Paul Zak (2017) compared with people at low-trust companies, people at high-trust companies report 74 percent less stress, 106 percent more energy at work, 50 percent higher productivity, 13 percent fewer sick days, 76 percent more engagement, 29 percent more satisfaction with their lives, and 40 percent less burnout.

Trust is not random, nor given automatically. There are always reasons why the trust level is where it is at in an organization. Identifying the behaviors that build trust and the behaviors that hurt trust is a valuable activity for any OD practitioner. While identification is the first step, the real challenge lies in reducing or eliminating harmful behaviors and maximizing helpful behaviors. This is the work of everyone within the organization starting from the top down. There has been significant research into the importance of trust and volumes written about the benefits of trust, including less turnover, fewer lawsuits, higher levels of productivity, more creativity and innovation, etc. According to an O. C. Tanner global culture report (2020), when employees have high levels of trust with their leaders, there is a 250 percent increase in the probability of reporting a constructive organizational culture. The building of a trusting environment and relationships may be the most important task any OD practitioner has.

For most individuals, trust is built slowly, over time, and with repeated consistent behaviors. One of the few times trust can be built instantly is in a crisis; otherwise building trust tends to take time. An individual becomes trustworthy when they are consistent and reliable. Losing trust, however, can happen in an instant, especially if the act or behavior was egregious. Once lost, it is terribly difficult to reestablish the trust back to the same level it was before it was lost. There are some who believe it cannot ever be reestablished back to the same level it was previously. They have a phrase: "Trust is established once and lost once." Often, when trust is lost, it is not the egregious behaviors but the tiny seemingly insignificant behaviors repeated over time that causes one to lose trust in another. Death by a thousand tiny papercuts. Examples include constantly being late, not keeping time commitments, telling people you will get back to them and then forgetting to do so, talking negatively about someone behind their back, being hateful and constantly negative, being highly judgmental and critical, etc. Trust is perishable for some and reinforcing for others.

There are both areas of trust and levels of trust to consider. I may trust you at work, to deliver what you say you will, but not trust you enough to take a vacation with you. I may trust you a lot in one area of life and not at all in another area. Some people trust everyone more easily, while others are more cautious. Your life experiences are probably the major influencers in how quickly and how deeply you trust others.

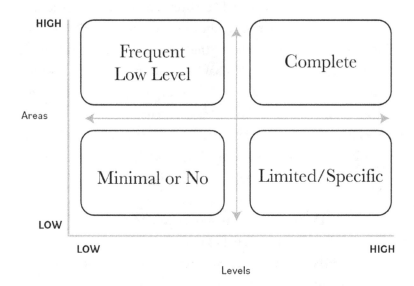

Complete trust in others is rare and is usually more frequent in one's more intimate relationships. Average trust is probably found in most organizations, which, unfortunately, is often reported as high levels of trust by the individuals. To develop high levels of trust, your knowledge of the individual usually extends beyond the workplace through additional socialization and activities. When there is no opportunity for these experiences to take place, then a part of each person's life is unknown to others and makes it difficult if not impossible to trust someone in areas you know nothing about. Further, there are many studies analyzing which professions are trusted the most and least. Consultants are rarely listed in either category. More research will need to be done to determine the trust reputation of consultants in general and OD practitioners specifically.

ASSESSING TRUST

Assessing the trust level in an organization is both easy and simple. One merely needs to ask the employees of that organization to pick a number between one (low) and ten (high) reflecting the current trust level and write it down. Add up everyone's number divided by the number of respondents to get the average, plus you will have high and low scores, enabling you to see the range. While the numbers are telling, they are not necessarily what is important. What is important are the behaviors that are responsible for the numbers. The next step would be to ask the employees to build two lists, one list to identify all the behaviors that help to build trust and the second list to identify all those behaviors that hurt trust. They usually will have a decent list. There are several next steps that can be powerful.

- Link all the behaviors, both supportive and non-supportive, with their organizational values.
- Decide how they are going to handle behaviors that hurt trust going forward.
- Have each natural work team commit to increasing the frequency of those behaviors that help build trust.
- Then for the next several months have each team review progress. This is a simple yet powerful intervention.

Assessing the trust level, the readiness to deal with difficult issues, the willingness to be candid and forthright, to be open in their communications, to deal with conflict in a healthy manner, and to be introspective are all important elements of working with groups. There is an interesting dynamic regarding communications. When a group is ready to address an issue, they will constantly come back to that issue until it is brought out and discussed, and if they are not ready to talk about it, they will dance all around the agenda until it is time to go home.

TEAMBUILDING

Before investing time, money, and energy into any team-building initiative, the first step is to identify if a collection of people is a team or a group. There is a significant difference, and it makes no sense to attempt team building with a group of individuals that are not a team. If it is a group and not a team, then team bonding may be more appropriate than team building. A group of individuals (usually three or more) may have a few common elements such as one boss they all report to or situated in their own department and sit in proximity to one another, etc. If their work, however, is not dependent on one another, there is no interdependence. There is no reason for them to collaborate or even cooperate. They can work independently and get their own work accomplished without any support from others. This is a group where bonding efforts may be more appropriate than team building.

There are times when a workgroup is already performing effectively and has no need or desire to develop further. From an organization design perspective, if the group has the right mix of positions to effectively perform the work of the group and accomplish its goals, and are collegial or at least have surface harmony, then there may be no need for any further interventions. This may be especially true if the group also has no desire to change what they already have and improve their processes.

On the other hand, a team is an interdependent group, and for the work to get done, each member must contribute their piece. The more support of one another and collaboration with one another, usually the better the team performs. A group may be more like a baseball team wherein each member can operate independently. For instance, when the batter is up at the plate, the other team members can only watch and cheer. Similarly, when the ball is hit to the outfield, all the other players can do is watch and hope someone catches it. They only have to work together when they have to throw someone out at a base. Whereas in a football team, every play for both sides depends on all other players doing their part. Football is more of a team sport and baseball a group sport.

Team building is a process that helps teams mature (Tuckman, 1965), develop a common goal, become more unified and collaborative, enhance communications, trust, and openness, and improve their processes and group dynamics for enhanced performance.

Team bonding is a process that focuses on bringing people closer together through improved interpersonal relationships, building trust, getting to know one another, and learning to care for each other and is typically not as concerned about performance issues. Team bonding is more concerned about behavioral issues and relationships. Some activities like conflict resolution can be appropriate for either team building or team bonding initiatives.

Often the two activities, team building and team bonding, take place at the same time, but they can be separated and should be when appropriate.

TEAM BONDING	TEAM BUILDING
Building relationships	Improving performance
Communication	Cooperation
Building Trust	Dependability
Spending time together	Working toward a common goal
Getting along with one another	Getting work accomplished with one another

Building a better team (team building) or a more self-directed or higher performing team usually takes considerable time and multiple meetings. During that process, it is quite common to expect a number of non-productive meetings as the membership struggles with the changes. These non-productive meetings are a natural step in the process of improvement but are often seen by the employees as a waste of time, and then there is a danger of the group giving up and merely focusing on the tasks required of them and not the process improvement, which can seem nebulous at times. It is those waste of time meetings that cause enough discomfort to move the group to new behaviors and are both necessary to and critical in the change process (*Tavistock* approach). However, a group can get stuck in unproductive meetings, and that is where the skilled OD practitioner can intervene and provide support and facilitation.

GROUP DYNAMICS

Every group has a process, whether it is known or not. Most groups have an informal process while some groups establish a more formal one, such as Robert's Rules of Order. The process naturally affects everything the group does and therefore its productivity or output. Included in the process might be such elements as the following:

- How the group communicates both internally and externally
- How the group makes decisions
- Use of authority and who has it
- Membership and inclusion criteria
- How the group handles conflict
- Stages of group development
- Expected attitudes
- Problem-solving processes
- Formal and informal behavioral patterns
- Rituals
- Rules, regulations, and policies that are adopted
- Dress codes
- Compliance to group norms, pressure to conform, group thinking
- Relationships
- Group size
- Trust levels
- Group emotions

Helping a team improve its performance generally means focusing on the group's dynamics and process. The practitioner, through their facilitation skills and awareness of group dynamics, often is in a position to help groups improve.

Much has been written about the importance of group dynamics ever since the Hawthorne studies of the 1940s as well as the contributions of Kurt Lewin, who first used the term "group dynamics." Lewin posited that changing individual behavior was almost impossible since every individual was influenced by group peer pressure, norms, values, culture, etc. Schein in 1988 talked about creating a disequilibrium within the culture to facilitate change behaviors.

Lawrence Kohlberg's (1958) "four stages of moral development" said that there were stages above the group norms, called post-conventional, wherein an individual decided what is right for themselves. Stephen Covey in *The 7 Habits of Highly Effective People* (2004) said essentially the same thing in that he encouraged people to develop their own mission statement and values in life, specifically, habit one, "Be Proactive," and habit two, "Begin with the end in mind." So, whether you believe you can facilitate change in an individual's behavior or that change must come through changing the group's norms, values, processes, etc., you are dealing with the strong influences of upbringing, organizational, or group systems. Group dynamics is a rich field and is very telling (diagnostic) about the organization's culture.

Assessing the trust level, the readiness to deal with difficult issues, the willingness to be candid and forthright, to be open in their communications, to deal with conflict in a healthy manner, and to be introspective are all important elements of working with groups. There is an interesting dynamic regarding communications, and that is when a group is ready to address an issue, they will constantly come back to that issue until it is brought out and discussed, and if they are not ready to talk about it, they will dance all around the agenda until it is time to go home.

OD PRACTITIONER ROLES

What role(s) is the skilled OD practitioner expected to have during any change process? Senior executives and key stakeholders may not understand what organization development is and what it can do for the organization. Nevertheless, they will still have expectations of the practitioner. Often, OD is thought to be part of human resources or training and development, and organizations will add these duties to the practitioner's responsibilities. Adding other duties to the OD position ultimately dilutes the OD role and unknowingly minimizes OD's effectiveness. It is critical to get your role and the corresponding expectations clearly agreed to upfront and ensure those expectations remain the same once formally accepting the role. As a practitioner, you are responsible for determining, in conjunction with the client, what role you are expected to be in at any given time. Role clarity between practitioner and client can greatly influence the success or outcomes of a project.

Even after an excellent data gathering and diagnosis is complete, the role the OD practitioner believes necessary may not be what others are expecting or wanting. When these different expectations go unmet, disappointment ensues. For example, the client may expect that you will facilitate their meetings, but your expectation is to build a self-directed team. In a case such as this, the client is being dependent on the practitioner for facilitation while the practitioner is letting them struggle and not facilitating in order to allow group members to step up and provide the necessary leadership to be self-directed.

There are many roles the OD practitioner can occupy, and the role will likely change throughout the initiative or by group. Some teams may legitimately be more dependent on the practitioner, and others may only need a little guidance and then can be left alone. Although listed here in a linear fashion, the roles frequently blend with one another, often moving from one role to another and in some cases very rapidly. Here are a few common roles OD practitioners occupy:

- Observer. Views and reports but does not participate. This is a fairly simple role with minimal responsibility. Observe the group and report objectively and candidly what you are finding. This role is often used in conjunction with improving group process or in group conflict resolution.

- Coach. Someone who supports specific learners or clients in achieving goals. Coaching has become a cottage industry all in itself, and there are now many certified coaches. There are performance coaches, sports coaches, life coaches, executive coaches, financial coaches, etc. When providing coaching, matters often turn personal, and the OD practitioner needs to be aware of any potential conflict of interest issues or role conflict issues. Coaching is often a part of a change initiative.

- Mentor. A wise and trusted counselor or teacher, a supporter. This role is often used in conjunction with building an internal support system or an infrastructure that can support the change initiative once your responsibilities have been completed. This role will likely fall upon the internal practitioner more so than the external practitioner.

- Consultant/Advisor. A person who gives others advice or recommendations. Often the practitioner is asked for their advice or recommendations. There may be times when it is appropriate to give recommendations and at other times not (coaching, facilitating, teaching roles). Advising is more involved in the problem role than consulting. Advising is offering an opinion, making recommendations, whereas consulting, while it may include advising, can include facilitating, giving feedback, or coaching.

- Facilitator. A person responsible for leading or coordinating the work of a group. An important role discussed in more depth below.

- Problem Solver. A person who others depend on to fix issues or solve problems. Short term, on a specific issue this role can be very appropriate and appreciated, but long term, if the practitioner solves all of the problems, then the organization may not take the responsibility for those issues and the systems and processes do not fundamentally change and it will increase dependency on whoever is in that role.

- Partner. A person who shares responsibility or is associated with another. This role indicates ownership in the problem, process, or organization. To be an accomplice in a venture or a colleague of equal rank, the OD practitioner may partner with an external training organization to present an internal training program.

- Director. A person who controls or directs the affairs of a group or organization. This role assumes that the person has the authority to make decisions, provide direction, and give orders. This role puts the practitioner in a position of responsibility to ensure results and should be carefully entered into.

- Teacher. A person who educates or instructs others. A common role for practitioners. This is an ongoing and almost daily role for most practitioners. We are constantly developing others in an effort to lessen dependency on the practitioner.

- Strategist. An expert in strategy. Thinking ahead, looking for the root cause, developing staff, providing leadership development, looking for potential unintended consequences are all a part of this role and is an ongoing process for the practitioner.

Your role in the organization and on the project will likely be fluid and changing. If you are an external practitioner, you will likely be coming in as an authority figure and everyone within the organization will have their respective reactions to that authority. If you are internal, your authority may depend on who you report to in the organization. Generally, at the beginning of any engagement, there is more dependence on the OD practitioner for guidance, direction, advice, facilitation, and information. That initial dependence is generally appropriate, but as time goes on, the OD practitioner recognizes that continued dependence does not help to develop the team or organization and instead works to help the client to be more independent and self-sufficient. This process can be difficult, as it is often easier for staff to let someone else handle everything and avoid taking any responsibilities.

There may be times when you recognize and allow a certain dysfunction to occur in the effort to get others to step up and provide leadership, and as result, you are criticized for not facilitating better or allowing that dysfunction to continue. To the contrary, there may be times when you are leading an initiative and are criticized for not having others do that activity. It is a bit of a dance on knowing when to let go and encourage self-sufficiency, but in any case, that activity of helping the organization be self-sufficient begins the moment you are engaged.

FACILITATION, COACHING, ADVISING

The facilitating, coaching, and advising roles can easily blend with one another during any implementation process. Facilitation can be divided into content facilitation and context facilitation. Content facilitation is most often used to help a group solve problems and obtain results (very close to the problem-solving role). It is more goal or task oriented. Context facilitation helps the group or team increase awareness and skill in their own group process; it is more focused on group internal dynamics and maturation levels. Context facilitation helps the group better understand their own processes. Both are important skills for the practitioner.

Knowing how to be a good facilitator and being one are different. One is awareness and knowledge, and the other is skills and experience. A good facilitator is often a neutral third party who is not a team member and has no vote. When a team member facilitates, they most likely will go in and out of their facilitation role or can appoint another person to facilitate when the issue concerns them or their team. Without excellent facilitation skills, it is unlikely that any OD practitioner will be successful simply because they are frequently leading or being involved in meetings. It is important to be skilled in areas such as the following:

- Setting up a meeting
- Setting up a room
- Decision-making models
- Dealing with disruptive people
- Establishing agendas and goals
- Establishing ground rules and norms
- Facilitating healthy conflict resolution
- Determining optimal group size
- Building group trust
- Building positive interpersonal relationships
- Controlling a meeting
- Roles in a meeting
- Breaking deadlock in meetings
- Getting the dialogue going
- Remaining neutral and objective
- Preparing a reasonable agenda and sticking with it

By no means is this an exhaustive list, but it is an exhausting list. The only way to acquire all these skills is to facilitate hundreds of groups and learn from them all.

As important as all of the above roles are, there is probably no greater role or responsibility than ensuring both physical and psychological safety. When physical safety is a concern, there are generally other individuals or other departments, such as security, HR, building maintenance, that can be of assistance, and naturally this then becomes the first or top priority. When psychological safety is the issue, the practitioner may find themselves alone in a group fighting to keep the environment a safe place for all participants. This may include such activities as the following:

- Keeping confidences
- Stopping personal attacks
- Reducing or addressing intense emotions
- Stopping threatening or nasty language
- Stopping behaviors that induce fear
- Speaking truth to power
- Demonstrating healthy conflict resolution
- Welcoming everyone's voice regardless of their role in the organization
- Encourage honest and candid discussion

NOT SAFE

A client requested conflict resolution with one of their units of about forty people. The resolution efforts were to be with the eight managers/supervisors who had several argumentative subgroups but were in unity in hating the director. This conflict had been brewing for several years, and opinions were firmly held by all. This was to be a two-day event run by one of our conflict resolution-certified individuals and another consultant who was not experienced in dealing with conflict. As the session evolved, the issues came out, and then the blaming, finger pointing, and defensiveness arose. That should have been the first clue that the process was not experienced as safe nor as productive. As the accusing and defensiveness increased, so did the emotional intensity to the point where people were standing up and getting into each other's personal space. The entire environment became hostile and unsafe, and yet the two facilitators encouraged more issues to get out on the table. By noon, one person walked out of the room, never to return, the director left saying she was going to sue the organization and all involved were angry with one another, the consultants, and the process.

Not only did these consultants fail to keep the environment a safe place, but due to their ineptness, they helped to create a hostile environment and increase the conflict. They lost control of the room and the process. The client appropriately asked that these two individuals never come back to their organization. It took us several months to rebuild our trust level with the client and get back on track. The conflict resolution specialist believed he was following the model but was not sensitive to the participants (discussed elsewhere in this book) and lacked the necessary facilitation skills. He may have had knowledge of a model but not the skill to implement successfully.

How do your own values, upbringing, and paradigms affect how you facilitate? How strong are your values and beliefs? What are your core assumptions about people, communications, or teams? How strong is your desire to control or be center stage? Are you more task or people oriented? All these issues and many more affect your facilitation style. Being a skilled and artful facilitator requires both knowledge and experience. Much has already been written about facilitation, most notably Carter McNamara's *Consulting and Organizational Development*; Roger Schwarz and Anne Davidson's *The Skilled Facilitator's Field Book*; *The Skilled Facilitator*, also by Roger Schwartz; *and The Complete Facilitator* by Howick Associates. All are good places to start.

A word of caution, however, the more you facilitate for the client, the more dependent they are on you. The goal is always to be working yourself out of a job. So in addition to being a skilled facilitator, you might also be in a training or coaching role, helping the client learn the skills to self-manage their groups and meetings.

TRAINING AND DEVELOPMENT

The OD practitioner wisely needs to be careful when providing T&D activities. When T&D is used appropriately, it benefits the organization, improves the skills, knowledge, and capabilities of the employees, and improves the overall organizational performance. If people lack knowledge or skills, that is when training is most appropriate. If it is a behavioral issue, then it may not be a skill issue, but a motivational issue or a systems influence issue. If the system and behaviors need to be addressed, then OD is the appropriate intervention. There will be many opportunities to provide training in combination with other organization development activities. Developing needed task-oriented skills will also inevitably help the group develop as well.

There is much already written about adult learning principles and many good instructors. It is not the intent of this work to review what is readily available. However, whether the OD practitioner is providing the instructions themselves or hiring or partnering with a trainer, it would be nice to know what differentiates a good trainer from an average or below-average trainer. In general, there are three characteristics of a good instructor:

- Reasonable content knowledge: they know their topic well.
- Reasonable platform skills: they have good instructional capabilities and can read group dynamics well and can control the learning environment.
- They live the material; they walk the talk. This is by far the hardest characteristic to develop.

All training programs hopefully benefit or improve both the individual and the organization. This means it is also important to be able to measure improvement based on a specific training program. Donald Kirkpatrick's (1994) four-level evaluation method has enjoyed popularity in the training and development field. The four levels of evaluation are:

- Participant reaction: usually accomplished by program evaluations.
- Learning: often measured with before-and-after tests or other demonstration of learning.
- Behavior: changes in behavior can be observed by others.
- Results: often measured against a previously identified outcome.

While many organizations want to know what the return on investment would be for providing the training (level four), most organizations do not want to go through the trouble, time, and expense of collecting statistics before and after the training program, so the ROI is often difficult to determine. Even level three takes observation and reporting by a third party and often goes unchecked. It is difficult to find companies that have calculated their ROI for training and development efforts, and yet according to the Association for Talent Development (ATD) (2018), American companies spent on training an average of $1,200 per employee in 2018. More and more organizations are seeing the need to invest in human capital, and providing training programs is a major contributor to that effort. Organizations have realized that while training may be expensive, the costs of ignorance are even higher.

There is another issue to consider regarding training: the quality of the training. There is still a significant amount of training that is substandard and does not follow adult education principles. These programs tend to have minimal value and, in the worst case, may be a waste of time and money. There are many reasons for this substandard training. Among them are the following:

- After the training, there is no follow up or reinforcement of any kind
- No expectation that the training be used
- Poor trainers
- Poor program design and delivery
- Terrible learning environment
- Participants forced to attend
- Not relevant to participants' current job

DOES TRAINING REALLY BENEFIT THE ORGANIZATION?

All too often the answer to a problem in an organization is a training program. Once that decision is made, then significant efforts go into designing the best training program possible.

- Will this be mandatory or volunteer training?
- Who will be the target audience?
- Where will it be held?
- When is the best time to accommodate everyone's work schedule?
- Who will teach the material?
- Will this be interactive or more information sharing?
- How long will the training be?
- What follow-up will there be?
- What will be the content and sequence of delivery?
- Will we use PowerPoints and videos or not?

However, the question really is, is training the solution to our problem? Is this a skills issue that would benefit from training or is this a process or behavioral issue that would better benefit from a different intervention? Maybe it is a leadership issue or a systems issue.

Too many times we have seen training programs implemented to fix some organizational problem only to fail to fix the problem, and that is because it was never a training issue in the first place. Then, when training fails to fix the problem, training or the trainers are often blamed for the failure. By fixing blame on some external factor, leadership never has to look internally at their decisions. Further, the employees who were sent to the training become even more jaded toward any future training programs. It is a downward negative cycle.

Training is an extremely valuable part of many, if not most, organization improvement initiatives. Without a doubt, training is helpful and has its place, but it is not the cure-all to everything. Do your diagnostic work first to determine root cause and identify all the elements that contribute to the problem and then determine if, when, and where, in the corrective process, what training is appropriate. If you provide the world's best training, hosted by a fantastic trainer, and the participants learn a lot, but you put them back into the same system that produced the problem behavior in the first place, employees will revert back to what the system supports and encourages. Training by itself is rarely the solution, but training in conjunction with other initiatives is often recommended.

Once you determine that training is appropriate, then design the delivery of the program to have maximum benefit. Make the training a part of a process and not a standalone event. You do this by requiring pre- and post-work and following up on the training. A great many of the training programs provided are not taught in a way that maximizes the learning opportunity. They do not incorporate the principles of adult learning or modern-day neuroscience. It is no wonder that learning retention is dismal. The primary way many programs are taught today, lecture, has the poorest retention rates. Arguably, lecture is said to have only a 5 percent retention rate in the learning pyramid. Then there is death by PowerPoints, which is also a popular method of instruction with up to a 20 percent retention rate.

Training that involves the participants and is highly interactive generally has the best learning retention. This involvement and interaction can be accomplished in many ways: movement by either the instructor or the students, varied teaching methods, multiple instructors, students teaching each other, hands-on experience, topic relevance, etc. Training is often designed to improve organizational performance or fix a problem, but some training is offered simply as a matter of employee development without a specific problem that needs solving. Employee development is often referred to as "education" and more future-oriented, while "training" often focuses more on the short term and on skill development.

There are additional benefits to training not necessarily a part of the program content or design such as the following:

- employees getting to know one another
- building relationships, networking
- building trust
- teambuilding
- improved creativity and problem-solving

These activities have a value all of their own and by themselves may be worth the training time; however, it might be better to find a way to promote these activities on an ongoing basis (a part of the infrastructure) rather than an occasional event.

DEVELOPING INFRASTRUCTURE

One might argue that the goal of all practitioners is to work themselves out of a job, to help the organization be independent and no longer need the services of the practitioner, especially if the practitioner is external to the organization. However, helping the organization be independent is a process that begins with the very first contact and is not always easily achieved. Many organizations and individuals would rather someone else take the responsibility for organizational improvement, especially when there are difficult, long-term problems to overcome. All this to say, there is a natural progression that typically takes place with most organizations.

In the beginning, there is a natural and important dependence on the OD practitioner as they have outlined a process for improvement, will direct and implement that process, are knowledgeable about the process, have the blessing of senior leadership, and are seen as an authority figure. In the beginning, they may be more direct and facilitate many meetings and discussions. Communication tends to be directed toward the practitioner, and their answers may mean more than peer answers at this time. Symbolically the group dynamic may look like this.

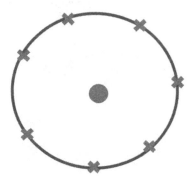

In this picture, you see the OD practitioner at the center of the group with the group dependent on their leadership/facilitation.

As the group matures and can handle more of the workload, the OD practitioner begins to reduce their leadership, facilitation, and participation and allow the group to take on as much as they can. There may be times when the practitioner has to jump back in the center to ensure success or progress, but they quickly go back to being more interdependent and more of a team member than a leader. Symbolically their role may look more like this.

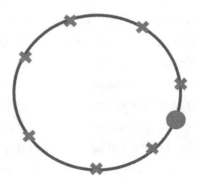

The final stage is independence where the practitioner is more of an observer and only advises or participates as minimally necessary, but mostly is encouraging and motivating the team/organization to do it on their own. Symbolically their role may look like this.

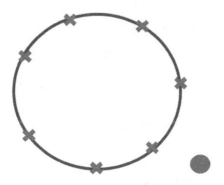

From the beginning, the OD practitioner, especially the external practitioner, realizes that it is not their organization and the senior leaders have the right and duty to reject any advice they feel is not in the best interest of the organization. Senior leaders have the right to make poor decisions, much to the dismay and angst of the practitioner, especially when the practitioner had advised them against it. Organizations will not always accept your suggestions or direction, and there will be times when what the senior leaders are proposing is going to do more harm than good and it is up to the practitioner to advise them accordingly. If the consequence of their decisions is damaging to the end goal of what the practitioner was charged with, then it may be necessary to revisit the contracting phase or decide whether to continue on at all.

Certainly, we have all seen programs or initiatives that were designed for a specific purpose, were delivered well, had good ratings by those involved, and yet nothing substantial changed within the organization. That is because the solution was not the solution.

DISCUSSION QUESTIONS

- Does your organization have a bias for action, or do they tend to carefully and thoroughly plan?
- Do you establish clear contracts for each initiative requested of you?
- How would you classify your organization's design?
- Would you consider your organization a continuous learning organization?
- How is the staff developed?
- Does training tend to be the answer to most problems in the organization?
- Which leaders are more task oriented and which ones are more people oriented?
- How would you classify your organization's leadership style?
- Do the decisions in your organization tend to be simple, system, or strategic?
- How often are there unintended consequences to the decisions in your organization?
- Which relationships are positive, and which ones are strained or worse toxic?
- Which leaders struggle at building relationships and which leaders have great relationships?

- Overall, how high is the trust level in your organization?
- Which departments/teams have low trust and why?
- Which teams/departments have high levels of cooperation (strong teams), which ones have surface harmony and just get along, and which ones are conflicted?
- Why do projects sometimes fail in your organization?
- Which roles do you tend to play in your organization?
- How effective are the training and development efforts in your organization?

CHAPTER SEVEN

The Future of OD

INTRODUCTION

Forecasting the future is difficult at best: the clues one might use are changing constantly and quickly, making any predictions something like weather forecasting: tricky and often limited in accuracy. Major clues might include wars, economic depressions, pandemics, global economy, tariffs and trade wars, and natural disasters. Has the current pandemic changed the nature of work permanently? Will more people work from their homes permanently? If so, how will this affect what OD practitioners will be requested to provide? Will the humanistic skills, i.e., collaboration, building trusting and positive work relationships, communications, developing and living by a set of values that respect humanity, team building, employee engagement, etc., be more or less important? Or will this cause managers and supervisors to be less humanistic and more focused on task accomplishment? Even more basic, if people are not working in a common brick and mortar facility, do we even have an organization, or do we have a loosely held entente?

For years, many have said the people skills (i.e., the soft skills) are the hard ones to implement. Process, system, and policy changes are relatively easy compared to building a high-performance team or resolving long-standing team conflict. Will the people skills be even more difficult to implement now that we are not physically close to one another? We all know that through social media it is easier to be rude, not care, and defriend someone, so how will this affect working relationships? How many people currently get on a group conference call and both mute themselves and do not press the video option so they cannot be seen or heard? What is the effect of this on building a cohesive team?

We believe that the skills the OD practitioner possesses will become even more valuable in the future but may not be immediately recognized by the organization. After all, work gets done through people, so people will remain important, and if there were no people, there would be no organization. The people skills will remain important, but the administration of those skills will likely be different as more and more workers are working remotely. Organizational systems, policies, and practices will likely change as well as more people work remotely, and their influence on human behavior will likely be different. The OD practitioner will need to be sensitive to those changes and adapt accordingly.

FACTORS INFLUENCING OD

People Analytics/Data

Modern human capital management efforts include a focus on people analytics. People analytics means an organization is using a data-driven approach to assessing, designing, and implementing human capital efforts that lead to organizational success (or goal achievement). People analytics involves a deep understanding of data gathering and analysis methods that will provide insights into human capital activities. To achieve this, there is a need for HR offices to use more technology that collects data and provides reporting capabilities. One goal in people analytics is to strategically align people strategies with business strategies.

OD practitioners are in a great position to bring curiosity and research questions that could influence the people analytics field. Practitioners have insights into what kinds of data may help provide baseline assessments of client culture and climate as well as identify performance metrics that may improve the measurement and ROI for any programs implemented. Also, OD practitioners may find it beneficial to partner with people analytics professionals in their client organizations. While these specialists may not be collecting data with the intent of using it for OD, there is an opportunity to leverage what is already collected for diagnostic and measurement efforts.

One people analytics activity that applies to OD is the "network collaboration analysis" where people analytics professionals can help map out the informal organization structures that result in organization performance. Either using surveys or scouring technologies used for communications, people analytics professionals can create a visual map that shows which employees connect and to what extent they connect with each other. By identifying the network, OD professionals can identify further areas for exploration about what drives certain collaborative networks in an organization. This would be an interesting addition to many OD diagnostic assessments.

Pace of Change

Read any literature about organizational change, transformation, talent management, leadership, or organization design and you are bound to find a statement asserting the "pace of change" is ever increasing. However, you will rarely see further analysis or description than this statement. We may all be assuming that the pace of change is faster than it ever has been and will continuously increase. If we look at technology, communication methods, and climate change, this is probably true. However, if you look at the challenges organizations face with climate, culture, behaviors, and relationships—all the specializations of OD— the organizations are not changing as fast. Generally, behavioral and organizational change lags technological change.

Generally, leaders recognize that technology causes a need for reskilling and impacts relationship dynamics (such as by moving employees to remote work locations); however, little has changed in the ways humans adapt their relationships and behaviors, and these adaptations do not happen at the same pace as other changes. Quite simply, humans are not naturally programmed to change as fast as technology changes. We must buy in to the benefits of change and assess the investments required to make changes before we pursue them. Therefore, we still talk about goals, action plans, and forming habits to make an individual change.

How does this apply to the OD practitioner? The job of changing climate and culture remains one that requires an investment of energy and resources. Change management efforts still happen systematically, and we understand that human adaptations will require longer than technological adaptations. In change management, practitioners may want to consider how much change needs to be managed versus organically happen. One desire of many leaders is to create organizations that can adapt to emerging needs as quickly as possible, so it will be important to determine how to build a climate, culture, and relationships that can accommodate rapid changes. Rapid adaptation generally requires significant effort, support, discussion, communication, and possibly building new infrastructure, policies, and processes. Even then you are still dealing with the natural resistance to change and new processes that the human brain exhibits as well as a healthy change in the organization's culture. Many elements would support rapid change and an agile organization, such as high trust levels, a positive attitude, good relationships, strong leadership, and a culture of continuous learning, to name a few.

Automation of Work

Automating work is inevitable. Organizations continue to find new ways to modernize work processes, programs, and technology to create efficiencies. Automation will impact and potentially eliminate many jobs. With the advent of robotic process automation (RPA), many jobs can be supplemented to eliminate routine or low complexity from the worker's responsibility. This kind of automation will generally serve as a supplement to humans. However, social or collaborative robotics, where robots learn from human interaction and data, could result in the elimination of jobs. The spectrum of automation available means many, if not all, jobs will be impacted by automation technology. But what does this mean for organizational culture and behaviors?

The impact on the nature of work, including reduction of routine tasks, may likely result in changes to work processes. Changes in work processes may then result in teams interacting differently. Additionally, interdependencies between people and teams may increase or decrease because of automation. Thus, automation will change the way we need to think about describing and integrating jobs, work units, and technology to support the outcomes an organization is seeking. All these changes will potentially require OD practitioners to be sensitive to the changing nature of work, jobs, and interactions in organizations. Also, OD practitioners may want to proactively engage with their clients to highlight the culture changes that may result from implementing technology and automation into an organization. By creating awareness of the cultural impact of automation, OD practitioners can help prepare the workforce to effectively adapt their culture, climate, and behaviors to the changes.

Reskilling

As noted, automation will change the nature of work for many jobs, which may result in the need to reskill an existing workforce. If technology changes jobs occupied by many people, the organization may need to reskill a large portion of the workforce. Reskilling will then essentially become a change initiative, which could mean culture, climate, and communication will be impacted by the new technology. When all of these organizational systems or elements change, then leadership will also need to change. OD practitioners can be well positioned to support multiple stakeholders through a reskilling initiative.

Less Human Interaction

Automation, especially the kind that gives employees the capability to work remotely, may inevitably result in less interaction with humans. As we write this book, the majority of telework-capable employees are working from home due to the COVID-19 pandemic. Meetings are now largely held via platforms like Zoom™, Microsoft® Teams, and Adobe® Connect™. People are rapidly adapting to this kind of workforce and subsequently, learning the advantages and disadvantages of this kind of environment.

For some, working remotely is a blessing. There is more uninterrupted time available to execute work assignments, and there is the enjoyable feeling of working from home. For others, there is now a sharp increase in meetings every day and almost no available time to work through tasks. In between those two extremes, many people find themselves happy to have more time to execute work assignments but, at the same time, feel disconnected from their colleagues. This last group of employees highlights a significant challenge of virtual work environments. How do organizations create a culture of trust and collaboration with limited human interaction? How do organizations develop the next generation of managers, supervisors, and leaders if they have had limited human interaction? After all, we lead people and manage things.

OD practitioners should consider the virtual work environment when planning activities for a client. Consider, can a group intervention be done virtually, or must it be done in person? What about a mix of in-person and virtual activities? Can a client organization feasibly recall all employees to one physical location for activities? Should interventions focus on leaders' abilities to manage employees that work remotely? These questions will be answered based on the client's unique situation and capabilities. OD practitioners will need to be technologically competent to provide interventions and activities that can be hosted in the different varieties of virtual and in-person settings and that impact organizational culture and climate. Additionally, OD practitioners may want to familiarize themselves with the different varieties of collaboration platforms (e.g., digital whiteboards) that can be used when working with groups that have remote employees.

CHANGE IN WORLD VIEW

The traditionalist generation either went through the Great Depression (1929–1939) or were raised by parents who did, and work before play was a common paradigm. Concerns about jobs and security were the norm. Baby boomers were not as concerned about safety; they were living in "good times." Work was plentiful and incomes were improved. Millennials are often thought of as being more open minded and more supportive of diverse communities evidenced by their advocating for gay rights and equal rights for minorities. They also are often referred to as more narcissistic, wanting more "me" time both at home and work. Generation Z (1995–2015), the electronic generation, has spent more time on social media and with social issues. Many young people today are not as concerned about individual survival as the traditionalist might have been, but with global and social justice issues that affect their quality of life.

There are many movements today that are challenging the old status quo. There is increasing focus on sustainability, net-zero economies, circle economics, organic foods, social justice, the #MeToo movement, diversity and inclusion, and others, pushing employees to challenge their organizations to be better, to get involved. The generations today are looking for their organizations to be an instrument for social change and forcing organizations to have a broader, more global perspective. They are also searching for work to bring more of a sense of purpose to their lives. This is evidenced by the rise of positive psychology and its application to work, which leads to the building of positive environments, corporations, and even flourishing cities.

What, then, are the implications or obligations for the OD practitioner? If you are an internal (may also apply to external) consultant and your company is more singularly focused (internal on company improvements), do you have an obligation to encourage a broader perspective? What if your organization is focused on profitability, efficiency, customer service, and employee well-being, and not focused on any global issues? Furthermore, what if your organization is comfortable with where they are and see no need for change? These, and many others, are questions current and future OD practitioners will be confronted with.

Many OD practitioners have spent their entire lives studying system change, and now we might be saying that is not enough—you need a global perspective, a political or governmental perspective, as well as a social justice perspective. If this is the case, then what changes in academic curriculums need to be made? What changes in leadership mindsets, corporate cultures, mission statements, and the like need to be changed? Does the OD practitioner have an obligation to lead their clients in these directions, or to increase the client's awareness of these issues, or to encourage employees of the organization to have a more global perspective if the organization itself is not aware of these issues?

What if I am a younger OD consultant working with a one-hundred-year-old company that may still be polluting the environment for the sake of profit or has no sustainability plans? This is where the understanding of self is critical. What are your values, biases, and moral beliefs? Are you there to impose your own values and goals or to help the organization implement theirs? What if you help the organization raise their awareness of these global concerns and the organization essentially says, "No, thank you, we have too many other things to worry about," or they are a government organization with rules that might prohibit them from taking sides on a political issue?

Many small and mid-size organizations are in search of survival, not in search of excellence, and they certainly do not have a global or planet-wide perspective. If our mission is to help both individuals and organizations be better (a definition of OD proposed earlier in this book), do we now need to add "help the world be a better place"?

WHAT DO YOU THINK WOULD HAPPEN IF. . .

A company asked for your help with merging several departments, helping shift the culture from a non-collaborative one to a highly collaborative culture, improve relationships, build trust, and review all policies or procedures that might interfere with these initiatives. All laudable goals.

You then said, "Great, I can do that, and in addition, I will help you reach zero emissions in five to ten years and shift your procurements over to circle economics and increase your involvement in social justice issues around the world. However, the budget I require will need to increase, maybe significantly."

The question is do organizations exist to serve customers, to provide a healthy working environment for all employees, and as an economic engine for the community and nation, or to influence social justice and change? We can confidently say that there is a high possibility of uncertainty in the future. The environment will evolve, the generations are different, and OD as a profession will no doubt continue to evolve to meet the future needs of both people and organizations. OD practitioners will continue to be sensitive to the changing tides and navigate the social environment at the time in which they are practicing. There is no crystal ball telling us where the lens will focus in the future, but OD practitioners will benefit if they maintain the ability to adapt and help organizations navigate challenging social times as they arise.

BRIDGING THE GAP: ACADEMIA AND PRACTITIONERS

Currently, universities offering advanced degrees in organization development vary considerably in their approaches, with some emphasizing global initiatives, others with a stronger emphasis on research or empirical studies, and yet others on areas such as international studies, humanitarian needs, and organizational or political systems. Universities do an excellent job at providing the necessary knowledge that any practitioner will ultimately need but often fall short at giving the students the practical application and experience that will develop the student into a skillful practitioner. There is a great difference between being a knowledgeable and skillful practitioner. Generally, the only way to gain skills is with experience in applying the knowledge. A stronger partnership between practitioners and academia would benefit all concerned. Requiring internships or providing class credit for working in the field would also help develop the necessary skills a practitioner will need. Job shadowing, mentoring, coaching, or other opportunities for students to gain real-world experience will help to develop the skills the practitioner will undoubtedly need.

Additionally, beyond growing practitioner skillsets, there is a need for leaders of organizations to become more aware of system influences, and it would be ideal to see more leaders with advanced studies in OD. While degrees such as MBAs help leaders understand organizations from a business perspective, OD provides them with a system and human perspective that is critical to their ability to lead an organization.

CONFUSION IN OD

Currently, there exists confusion in the OD profession around many issues, i.e., *is* OD a profession, a field of study, a career? What other professions are included in OD? Is OD a part of the business school, education, psychology, HR, change management, or other? What is OD and what is only a part of OD? As long as the confusion exists, we believe that the profession will suffer not only an identity crisis, but a crisis of perceived worthwhileness.

Many individuals claim that they do OD, and upon further discussion, they disclose that they do leadership training or team building or executive coaching, etc. While all of these may be an important part of an OD intervention, as a standalone service or initiative, they are not by themselves organization development. In discussions with many other practitioners, there is strong agreement that there is confusion about what OD is within the field itself, with clients, executives, even one's own bosses. One practitioner told us that there is so much confusion that they do not even use the term OD anymore when describing what they do.

Currently, there is no formal set of qualifications for an OD practitioner, no education requirement, no certification process, and no licensing requirement, so anybody can call themselves an OD practitioner. It is no wonder that the field has not established itself as a valuable organizational or community asset. This lack of credentialing has and continues to diminish the profession. The future of OD would be greatly enhanced if OD professionals could rally around one common set of guidelines, ethics, and competencies for practitioners. Self-regulation by current OD professionals would be an excellent form of growth and formalization for this profession.

CONCLUSION

This book was written with the intent to provide professionals who affiliate with the term "OD practitioner" some thoughtful considerations about engaging in the practice, the process, and the future of the field. We hope that this book creates conversation, thoughtful reflection, in-depth analysis, and interest in the continual evolution of OD. As long as there are organizations staffed with people, there is a need for OD.

DISCUSSION QUESTIONS

- How does your organization get data on human capital issues?
- What is the pace of change in your organization and how does it affect operations?
- How is technology affecting you?
- How do you engage in continual learning as a practitioner?
- What can you do to positively influence the field of OD?
- What do you think are other influences impacting the field of OD?
- What are your two to three biggest takeaways from reading this book?
- What will you do differently as a result of this book?

CHAPTER EIGHT

Wisdom Bits

INTRODUCTION

What follows are one-line, often simplistic, statements that reflect a deeper meaning or contain bits of wisdom within the field of organization development and change management. They are meant to raise awareness (inform) and help guide practitioner actions. While interesting to read, they are sometimes humorous, sometimes serious, and generally reflect the true world of OD consulting. Many of these terse statements are full of substance. Take number sixty-seven for example: people can sense your true intent, your motivation, your caring, or your lack of it. This follows the adage that "people don't care about how much you know until they know about how much you care." Once people know that you have their best interest at heart, they will tolerate a few mistakes in technique. They will be forgiving if you are not perfect. On the other hand, if your technique is perfect but your motivations are doubtful, you will be seen as duplicitous or as a charlatan, you will not be trustworthy, and ultimately you will fail. So, while number sixty-seven is only five words, it is a deep statement that could provoke deep introspection. How much do you care? Does it show or do you tell people?

The first widsom bit, "Change is often a messy process," is only six words but profound. An example of this is listed in the box below. Many times, we have seen clients expect a clean, mistake-free, simple-to-implement change process, one that is similar (cookie cutter) that can be implemented repeatedly by following these six or seven steps. At least that is what they read in a book somewhere or the model has six or seven steps. While the model may be cut and dry, the implementation (real world) is not. Helping clients understand that change is messy, that mistakes will be made, that the timing will be off, that they will run into obstacles that will have to be solved or change the direction of the program, is all to be expected and quite normal is incredibly valuable. So again, a terse statement full of real-world meaning. We encourage the reader to read each statement slowly and see what meaning it has for you and to highlight ones you want to work on for yourself.

EXAMPLE

Years ago, a client engaged us to help them with their culture. A diagnostic process was recommended for us to be able to understand the current climate and to understand the vision of where they would like to be. It was a conflicted culture starting with two of the senior leaders at the top who were in philosophical disagreement about most issues. In addition to many system issues that pushed people into certain behaviors, the relationships in most departments were needing a lot of attention. There was a great deal of learned helplessness, depression, people who have just given up and were there for a paycheck, complaining, and blaming, etc.

One of the consultants on our staff, who was used to delivering assessments or testing instruments that were cut and dry, was assigned to the client. This individual got caught up in the relationship issues, did not remain neutral, but instead took sides with one of the senior managers (because it fit their upbringing, values, and biases), overworked the report, and used up most of their funds in writing the report. The client called and complained about many things, and our boss labeled the client as a difficult client. By doing so, they were exacerbating the issues.

Many realities were overlooked, and a big opportunity was missed to further help this client.

1. The client was exhibiting the problem. This was an extension of their normal culture.
2. Everything is diagnostic, and this was a missed opportunity.
3. What part did we contribute to the problem?
4. The boss's frustration with the client was a large clue to what the staff experiences with management.
5. Our consulting department expected people to behave rationally, logically. This is what they were used to when delivering testing measurements. The seemingly illogical behaviors of the client were abnormal to the consultant but were merely normal client behavior for the OD practitioner.

In this case, not only was change messy, but unintentionally we found a way to contribute to their process and make it even messier.

WISDOM BITS

1. Change is often a messy process.

2. Mistakes will be made. That is normal. How you react to them is what matters.

3. You are always learning.

4. You do not have to have all the answers.

5. Stay away from blame. It is not helpful and is usually harmful.

6. Reserve judgment until all the facts are in or at least until you hear both sides to the story.

7. The client should have at least 51 percent of the responsibility.

8. Start anywhere, go everywhere.

9. Identify your own values and then live by them.

10. There is always a reason why the behavior or a situation exists.

11. Dysfunctional behavior is serving some function.

12. Diverse opinions add to the richness and creativity of the solution. Welcome people who see it differently.

13. To get to the root cause, you will need to look at the entire system.

14. The client has the right to reject your advice and approach.

15. Senior leadership must be involved and champion the initiative. Very little changes without their involvement.

16. Building trust in an organization is a high-leverage activity.

17. What the organization tolerates is what they end up with.

18. Information is everywhere, and the practitioner is always in an information-gathering mode.

19. You see and interpret everything through your own biases, so know what they are.

20. Senior leadership is always a part of the problem, and they are also always a part of the solution.

21. The leadership style has a profound effect on organizational culture.

22. The organization's culture is ubiquitous, cannot be easily seen, yet affects everything.

23. Optimists are a great source of motivation but may miss some realities, skeptics tend to see the difficulties but are hopeful, and cynics tend to only see the negative and unconsciously or consciously hope for failure.

24. Not every project/initiative will be successful.

25. Sustainability generally requires building an internal infrastructure so that the work can carry on once the practitioner leaves.

26. The OD practitioner will adopt many different roles on any one project.

27. There is no one right model for change or organizational design.

28. Work policies, practices, procedures, rules, culture, and history all have a profound impact on human behavior.

29. It is natural for people to resist change but not always healthy.

30. If you see it, smell it, sense it, or hear it, say it. Bring unspoken issues out for discussion.

31. You have influence. You make a difference.

32. Keep information confidential.

33. Be trustworthy.

34. Bring in talent/expertise you do not have.

35. Disclose any conflicts of interest.

36. Work yourself out of a job. Do not create dependency.

37. Speak truth to power.

38. Be candid and diplomatic.

39. Remember people are afraid of and resist the unknown.

40. Be flexible because the needs of the organization constantly change.

41. The agenda is never the agenda.

42. Sustaining the changes is often more difficult than implementing them.

43. Always develop support at high levels.

44. Your attitude matters. Be positive and enthusiastic.

45.   Be compassionate and caring.

46. Show respect in all that you do.

47. Celebrate success. Showcase others.

48. Create a sense of urgency regarding any changes.

49. Obstacles are to be expected.

50. Positive relationships are the key to change.

51. What failed before will fail again if there are no changes.

52. Are you contributing to the problem?

53. Delegate as much as you can.

54. The organization is your client, not individuals.

55. Problems are often solved at a level above the problem.

56. The easy solutions (quick fix) usually address the symptoms, not the root cause.

57. Build from strengths as often as you can.

58. Problems not dealt with soon become normal or a part of the culture, and then they become a problem that just will not go away.

59. Everything is interrelated. Everything affects everything else.

60. Small changes can produce big results.

61. Cause and effect may be separated by a lot of time.

62. Today's problems were yesterday's solutions.

63. Today is the future you imagined yesterday.

64. The harder you push, the greater the resistance to change.

65. The people who complain about the problem are contributing to the problem.

66. There are only two responses to every human behavior: encouragement or tolerance and extinction.

67. Intent counts more than technique.

68. People would rather be around optimistic people than negative people.

69. You cannot change others; you can only change yourself, and that is hard enough.

70. Every day everyone creates the culture and reinforces the systems.

71. An organization's culture is not random.

72. If you think you are a leader, but no one is following you, then you might just be out for a walk.

73. Every action you take or do not take has consequences.

74. If you feel a certain way in a situation, many others may as well.

75. Build a network of practitioners you can share and brainstorm with.

76. Decisions may have bad outcomes, but that does not mean it was a bad decision. Reassess and make a new decision.

77. Learn from your failures and broaden your knowledge base.

78. All organizations are perfectly aligned to get the results they get.

79. More of the same is not the answer.

80. What gets recognized and rewarded gets repeated.

81. A narrow perspective leads to simplistic solutions.

82. There are proactive and reactive managers, and their success rate differs.

83. Organizational growth requires change and adaptation.

84. Adaptation is more about making minor day-to-day changes than one big change.

85. You only see what you are looking for.

86. Very few people ever function at their full potential.

87. The OD practitioner's success is determined by the client's level of commitment.

88. The initial meeting between client and consultant is a strong indicator of how the project itself will go.

89. If an organization is a living, changing, interdependent ecosystem, then the OD practitioner's work is never done.

90. Your organization will never change unless the people in it change.

91. If there is no involvement, there is no ownership, and when there is no ownership, the greater the resistance to change.

92. The anticipation of unintended consequences reduces them.

93. Changing just one thing in an organization is like moving one piece on a chessboard. It completely changes both the landscape and the strategy.

94. Diagnostic information is data, not a conclusion or the outcome.

95. Change is a process, training an event; don't confuse the two.

96. If it is an emotional issue, logic will not prevail. Compassion and understanding will.

97. Specificity leads to goal attainment, while generality leads to goal failure.

98.   People behave in ways that the system encourages or incentivizes them to behave.

99.   Those individuals closest to the work generally know best how to improve the work.

100.   You never learn anything while talking.

Stories for Reinforcement

A Great Risk: Certified and Knowledgeable, Far from Skillful

During a multiple-year engagement with a mid-size client, there arose a need for conflict resolution in one of their units. Interpersonal relationships were toxic and destructive with many individuals hating their boss, who was demeaning and hostile toward the employees. In addition, several other employees did not like each other, causing subgroups to develop within a team of about twenty-five people who were interdependent with one another. There were a number of consultants that have facilitated conflict resolution sessions in the past with great success, but all were busy, so we extended our search to another of our Midwestern offices. A young man said he was certified in a particular approach to conflict resolution. He had been on a number of similar assignments for the Midwest office with apparently good results so we felt comfortable in engaging him for our client. In addition, one of our own PhD OD consultants was going to be in attendance with him while he conducted the workshop.

This was to be a two-day session with the first day devoted mostly to teaching the model by the consultant and only brief exercises to solidify the teaching points. Day two was to be devoted to working on the actual issues. At the end of the first day, there was some dissatisfaction at not being able to get into the issues, but that is to be expected. I asked the consultants if they wanted me to attend the last day to help out or provide reinforcement; however, I was requested to stay away since they thought it would be best to keep the same two people present. As you might imagine, that was a big red flag; however, I chose to honor their request and stay away. I was going to pay a big price for that decision.

Day two apparently began with a brief review of the model and then getting into the issues they had with the boss. People were eager to speak up and be candid. It became a bit of a back and forth with people making judgments about one another, blaming one another, criticizing one another, demeaning one another, etc. The process was not well controlled, the language had risen to a hostile tone, the accusations were many, and the personal attacks were frequent. This became a "let's gang up on the boss session" with an unsafe environment. By noon, the boss was in tears, one individual walked out, never to return, and another said they would sue the organization. The session ended early in the afternoon, and the report we got back from this certified individual was that it went well but there were a few hiccups.

Over the next few days, we learned the severity of what really happened. Then we had to move into recovery mode. The project director and I went back to their office and talked one on one with everyone to apologize and ask for their experience during the session and to mend fences. Additionally, we offered them a different training program at no expense to make up for the two unproductive days they had spent in conflict resolution (which resolved nothing and instead generated conflict). Both the PhD consultant and the certified conflict resolution person were asked not to return to this client and their respective bosses were made aware of this situation. Fortunately for us, many of the problems took care of themselves when the boss and one other individual both left that office and went elsewhere, but they never did get resolved.

While we as a consulting organization survived the debacle, it was not the quality of work that me or the project manager was happy with. While mistakes will be made on projects, I wished they would not have been such a big mistake.

Lesson learned. Just because your certified and knowledgeable does not mean your good or experienced (skillful).

The Value of the 80 Percent Concept

An organization of about four hundred people engaged us to help them with their process improvement initiative. For the first few months, we worked with the senior leadership to determine their goals. They were a fractured and siloed team, each more concern about their individual responsibilities than the overall health of the organization. One business unit (which recommended us) had already engaged in improving their own processes and were able to build considerable improvements. In other words, they were already far down the road and prided themselves on being far ahead of their colleagues.

It became apparent during a series of meetings with upper management that not everyone was on board with this process. Yes, there was verbal support, but what else were they going to say when the top boss was there and he wanted this program to go forward? He had great success with this approach in another unit he ran several years earlier. Now he wanted the same approach for his new division. So of course, there was verbal consensus, but we could tell early on that there were some cynics in the group and certainly even more skeptics.

The approach involved first working with senior leaders, which we were already engaged in. Second, training would be provided in the organizational model we were using to all four hundred employees. Finally, assistance would be provided to individual business units to help them discover and implement their chosen improvements. This seemed like a reasonable approach, with the exception that we did not have 80 percent of the senior leaders on board and we knew it. Repeatedly, we talk to the senior boss and he said that his people would eventually come on board because that is what happened at his last assignment. We were doubtful because we assumed the following breakdown:

- Two to three of the senior leaders were really on board.
- One or two leaders were definitely not on board.
- One to three of them were in a wait-and-see mode.

Against our better judgment, and with encouragement from the boss, we moved from the first to the second step, training all four hundred employees. This was a two-day program with a maximum of twenty-five in a group, so we had to conduct sixteen to eighteen programs within nine months, a decent challenge for our small firm since there was only two trainers of this program. All four hundred people received the training, and the internal psychologist who was our point person was disappointed that he was not doing all of this work.

Soon after the training was complete, two of the units began to engage in the process of improvement when suddenly the senior boss was removed by HQ and transferred to another unit. The new leader was one of the one to three individuals we identified as "wait and see." The result was the entire project got put on hold and eventually faded into the background and ceased to exist. They spent $1,000.000 on this effort only to see it stop.

Lesson learned is that we violated our own 80 percent rule and did not have sufficient infrastructure in place to carry on the process once our champion was gone. We could have saved the organization a lot of money and ourselves a lot of time if we simply resolved the hesitancy on the part of the senior leaders.

Illegal, Ethical, Immoral

A small boutique consulting firm received a referral call from the director of HR to work with an offshore oil supply company that provided products and services to the oil rigs in the Gulf of Mexico. The organization was small and had less than one hundred employees, but they were not functioning well and seemed to have low or poor efficiency, low morale, and a fair amount of conflict. The initial agreement was that consultants were contracted to spend three days with the organization conducting a diagnostic process. The process was intended to discover the employees' perspectives on all of the cited issues. At the end of that time, the consultants would return to home base, discuss, analyze, and write up a report, and provide recommendations for improving the organization, at which point they would return to the organization and provide the results to senior leadership and facilitate an action-planning session. All fairly standard work in a diagnostic phase of an organization improvement initiative.

The consultants began the process. They scheduled the interviews, traveled to the client location, and conducted a series of individual interviews and focus groups. The focus groups did not result in much information other than polite corporate rhetoric. The consultants began to wonder if they were not trusted even though they began each meeting explaining who they were, why they were hired, and what was going to happen with the information. The consultants were careful to cover the confidentiality statement as well. As it turned out, the employees did not trust one another and were quite hesitant to talk in front of each another.

Upon reflection, the consultants realized there were a couple of red flags that resulted in their current challenges.

- Red flag #1: The consultants did not talk directly to any of the owners prior to accepting this engagement. All conversation was with the HR director, who seemed anxious to have us come and implement the process.

- Red Flag #2: The consultants did not have any of the senior leaders scheduled for interviews. In retrospect, it appears that senior leadership was going along with the HR director's wishes and granting him the money and authority to proceed with us.

At the end of the first day, prior to leaving the organization, the consultants sat in a conference room and discussed the initial findings from the one-on-one interviews and focus groups. The information the consultants learned was not what they were prepared for, and it was not something that they were ever taught in school. The group sat there with jaws on the floor as they discussed their data. Things that consultants learned:

- One of the senior executives was also on a ghost payroll of the governor.
- Bribes to get contracts were a normal part of their business.
- They provided prostitutes to their buyers in order to get contracts.
- They would falsely bill clients' extra amounts when they could.

All of this information was in stark contrast to the normal low-trust levels, poor communication, competition among silos, everybody out for themselves, hostile communications when there was communications, etc.

After sharing the information amongst themselves, the consultants realized that there was nothing that they could do to help this organization. The client was not going to change the way they did business; they felt that this was their reality, the nature of the business they were in, that everyone does this, etc. The consultants also knew that it would be a waste of time and money to attempt to work with the staff since senior leadership modeled the opposite of everything that would be taught.

The consulting team brought the HR director in (they still had no access to the owners) and told him what was learned (he was amazed that we found this all out in one day) and that given the environment, anything they might do for him would not be sustainable, fail outright, be seen as duplicitous as long as the owners were the way they were, and be a waste of his money. The consultants said they were leaving and not coming back, and there would be no charge for the day. In the end, they could not ethically work for this company. Of note, the company went out of business several years later.

References

Association for Training and Development. *New ATD Research: Investment in Talent Development on the Rise* [Press Release], December 2018. https://www.td.org/press-release/new-atd-research-investment-in-talent-developcment-on-the-rise

Bass, B. M., & Riggio, R. E. *Transformational Leadership* (2nd ed.). Psychology Press, 2005.

Bauer, Taylor N. "Onboarding New Employees: Maximizing Success." The Society for Human Resources Management, 2010. https://www.shrm.org/foundation/ourwork/initiatives/resources-from-pasti-nitiatives/Documents/Onboarding%20New%20Employees.pdf?utm_source=link_wwwv9&utm_campaign=item_235121&utm_medium=copy.

Blanchard, K., Broadwell, R., & Maxwell, J. C. *Servant Leadership in Action: How You Can Achieve Great Relationships and Results* (1st ed.). Berrett-Koehler Publishers, 2018.

Boushey, Heather, and Sarah Jane Glynn. Center for American Progress, November 16, 2012. https://www.americanprogress.org/wp-content/uploads/2012/11/CostofTurnover.pdf

Brown, B. *Dare to Lead: Brave Work. Tough Conversations. Whole Hearts.* (First Edition). Random House, 2018.

Cracking the Code of Change. Harvard Business Review, July 13, 2015. https://hbr.org/2000/05/cracking-the-code-of-change

Covey, Stephen R. *The 7 Habits of Highly Effective People: Restoring the Character Ethic.* [Rev. ed.]. New York: Free Press, 2004.

Covey, S. M., Covey, S. R., & Merrill, R. R. *Speed of Trust: The One Thing That Changes Everything* (1st ed.). FranklinCovey, 2008.

Deloitte. *Rewriting the Rules for the Digital Age. 2017 Deloitte Human Capital Trends.* Deloitte University Press, 2017. https://www2. deloitte.com/content/dam/Deloitte/global/Documents/About-Deloitte/central-europe/ce-global-human-capital-trends.pdf

Dictionary.com, s.v., "bias." Accessed July 17, 2021. https://www.dictionary.com/browse/bias

Dictionary.com, s.v., "organization." Accessed July 21, 2021. https://www.dictionary.com/browse/organization

Dictionary.com, s.v., "system." Accessed July 17, 2021. https://www.dictionary.com/browse/system

Festinger, L. *A Theory of Cognitive Dissonance* (Anniversary ed.). Stanford University Press, 2021.

Fredrickson, B. *Positivity: Top-Notch Research Reveals the 3-to-1 Ratio That Will Change Your Life* (1st ed.). Harmony, 2009.

Galbraith, J., Downey, D., & Kates, A. *Designing Dynamic Organizations: A Hands-on Guide for Leaders at All Levels* (59392nd ed.). AMACOM, 2001.

Goleman, D. *Emotional Intelligence: Why It Can Matter More Than IQ* (10th Anniversary ed.). Bantam, 2005.

Hall, Jonathan, and Alan Kreuger. "An Analysis of the Labor Market for Uber's Driver-Partners in the United States," January 22, 2015. https://s3.amazonaws.com/uber-static/comms/PDF/Uber_Driver-Partners_Hall_Kreuger_2015.pdf.

Hogan, Maren. "9 Employee Retention Statistics That Will Make You Sit Up and Pay Attention." TLNT, November 30, 2015. https://www.tlnt.com/9-employee-retention-statistics-that-will-make-you-sit-up-and-pay-attention/.

Kilmann Diagnostics. December 24, 2020. https://kilmanndiagnostics.com/overview-thomas-kilmann-conflict-mode-instrument-tki/

Kirkpatrick, Donald L. *Evaluating Training Programs: The Four Levels.* San Francisco: Emeryville, CA: Berrett-Koehler; Publishers Group West [distributor], 1994.

Kotter, J. P. *Leading Change, With a New Preface by the Author* (1R ed.). Harvard Business Review Press, 2012.

Kouzes, J. M., & Posner, B. Z. *The Five Practices of Exemplary Leadership* (2nd ed.). Pfeiffer, 2011.

Lewin, K. *The Conceptual Representation and the Measurement of Psychological Forces* (Illustrated ed.). Martino Fine Books, 2013.

Mackenzie, A., & Nickerson, P. *The Time Trap: The Classic Book on Time Management* (Fourth ed.), 2009.

Maslow, A. H. *A Theory of Human Motivation.* Martino Fine Books, 2013.

McGregor, D. *The Human Side of Enterprise, Annotated Edition* (1st ed.). McGraw-Hill Education, 2006.

McKinsey & Company. *Enduring Ideas: The 7-S Framework*, 2008. Accessed July 17, 2021. https://www.mckinsey.com/business-functions/strategy-and-corporate-finance/our-insights/enduring-ideas-the-7-s-framework

Peters, T. J., & Jr., R. W. H. *In Search of Excellence: Lessons from America's Best-Run Companies* (Reprint ed.). Harper Business, 2006.

Peterson, C., & Park, N. Classifying and measuring strengths of character. In S. J. Lopez & C. R. Snyder (Eds.), Oxford handbook of positive psychology, 2nd edition (pp. 25-33). New York: Oxford University Press, 2009.

Peterson, C., & Seligman, M. E. P. Character strengths and virtues: A handbook and classification. New York: Oxford University Press and Washington, DC: American Psychological Association, 2004.

"Proof That Most Business Development Training Fails." BD Academy, February 1, 2021. https://bdacademy.pro/proof-traditional-bd-training-fails/.

Rogers, C., & M.D., P. K. D. *On Becoming a Person: A Therapist's View of Psychotherapy* (2nd ed.). Mariner Books, 1995.

Salovey, P., & Sluyter, D. *Emotional Development And Emotional Intelligence: Educational Implications* (Illustrated ed.). Basic Books, 1997.

Schein, E. H., & Schein, P. A. *Organizational Culture and Leadership (The Jossey-Bass Business & Management Series)* (5th ed.). Wiley, 2016.

Schein, E. *Process Consultation Revisited: Building the Helping Relationship (Pearson Organizational Development Series)* (1st ed.). Addison Wesley Longman, 1998.

Shewhart, W. A., & Deming, E. W. Statistical Method from the Viewpoint of Quality *Control (Dover Books on Mathematics)* (F First Edition). Dover Publications, 1986.

Taylor, F. W. *The Principles of Scientific Management.* Dover Publications, 1997.

Tuckman, B. W., & Jensen, M. A. C. Stages of Small-Group Development Revisited. *Group & Organization Studies,* 2(4), 419–427, 1977. https://doi.org/10.1177/105960117700200404

Versai, Anna. "Cost of Employee Turnover vs. Retention Proposition." The HR Digest, March 16, 2018. https://www.thehrdigest.com/cost-of-employee-turnover-vs-retention-proposition.

Walker, M. *Why We Sleep (Unlocking the Power of Sleep and Dreams)* (1st ed.). Scribner, 2017.

Walton, M., & Deming, E. W. *The Deming Management Method* (Illustrated ed.). Perigee Books, 1988.

Wigert, Ben, and Ryan Pendell. "7 Problems With Your Onboarding Program." Gallup.com. Gallup, June 25, 2021. https://www.gallup.com/workplace/247172/problems-onboarding-program.aspx.

Wyzowl.com "The Human Attention Span [INFOGRAPHIC]." Accessed July 5, 2021. https://www.wyzowl.com/human-attention-span/.

Zak, P. Harvard Business Review - Ideas and Advice for Leaders. *Harvard Business Review,* 2017. https://hbr.org/

About the Authors

Dr. Larry Kokkelenberg received his PhD in clinical and industrial psychology and has been consulting with organizations since 1970. He has worked in government, nonprofits, and private organizations from family-run businesses to Fortune 100 corporations.

Regan Miller, MS, is currently a team lead for the US Office of Personnel Management's (OPM) Workforce Planning and Reshaping Division within OPM's HR Solutions. In this role, she provides OD, organization design, and human capital management services to public-sector clients nationwide. Regan previously served in the private sector in training and development positions. Across her federal career, she has served in civilian positions within the Department of Army and the Defense Logistics Agency.

To contact the authors with general inquiries or questions about this book, please email accidentalpractitioner@gmail.com or visit www.otcwebsite.com

We want to hear your story!

Everyone has dozens of stories/experiences, both good and bad: a great boss, a terrible boss, great colleagues or terrible colleagues, a great working experience or a terrible working experience. There are endless examples of real-life experiences that we all can learn and benefit from, so we want to hear your story.

- Were you ever caught off guard by a request? Tell us about it!
- Were you ever handed an assignment you knew would fail or not help the situation?
- Have you ever run across an illegal or unethical situation?
- Have you ever had to work with someone that was an absolute disaster?
- Have you ever had to work for a boss and the boss was the problem? Tell us about it!
- Have you ever had a project fail or suddenly stop in the middle of implementation?
- Have you ever thought "not in my wildest dreams" and yet there you were?

- Have you ever had a client hand you a solution and yet they did not know what the problem was? Tell us what happened.
- Have you ever turned down an assignment and why?

GUIDELINES

- No more than three pages and one to two pages preferred. Multiple stories are welcomed.
- No individual or organization names.
- First, second or third person, all are acceptable.
- Does not have to be recent, any time period is acceptable.
- No profanity.
- We will edit for grammar only, but not content.

Send your story to accidentalpractitioner@gmail.com with your permission to use in our future publications. You will be acknowledged as the author if you desire, and if you do not want your name as author, we will protect that as well.

Submitting your story for inclusion in our forthcoming book indicates your permission to use your story now or in the future.